To truly follow Jesus you must adopt ... matters more than the kingdom of God! The kingdom... proactive, redemptive, creative, counterintuitive, positive, collaborative, comprehensive, transformative, and yes, subversive. I dare you to join the rebellion. This book will show you how!

Rick Warren
Saddleback Church
Lake Forest, California

In *Subversive Kingdom*, my friend Ed Stetzer introduces us to extraordinarily practical ways to make a lasting kingdom impact. Anyone desiring to make a redemptive difference in their world will find Ed's words both inspiring and instructional.

Andy Stanley
North Point Community Church
Alpharetta, Georgia

When God the Son was born Jesus the Christ, he established his kingdom and is now reconciling people, and eventually all things, to himself. *Subversive Kingdom* is a must read to understand the king, the kingdom, and our role as agents of God's kingdom. This book will help you join Jesus on his kingdom mission.

Matt Chandler
The Village Church
Highland Village, Texas

SUBVERSIVE

KINGDOM

SUBVERSIVE
KINGDOM

LIVING AS AGENTS OF
GOSPEL TRANSFORMATION

Ed Stetzer

PUBLISHING GROUP

NASHVILLE, TENNESSEE

978-1-4336-7382-5

Published by B&H Publishing Group
Nashville, Tennessee

Dewey Decimal Classification: 269.2
Subject Heading: CHRISTIAN LIFE \ EVANGELISTIC
WORK \ SPIRITUAL WARFARE

1 2 3 4 5 6 7 8 • 16 15 14 13 12

Dedication

To small church pastors

Who live as agents of God's kingdom every day, showing
and sharing the love of Christ in ways that don't get noticed
by many . . . except by Him who matters most.

Acknowledgments

Thanks to all those who helped on the journey of *Subversive Kingdom*, with ideas, comments, and editing. Thanks to John Shepherd, Philip Nation, Dino Senesi, and Trevin Wax for their input at different stages along the way. Thanks to Keith Whitfield who helped write and rewrite. Special thanks to Lawrence Kimbrough, an amazing editor who made *Subversive Kingdom* what it is today. Finally, thanks to all those who inspire us to kingdom living by sharing and showing the love of Christ every day.

Contents

PART I

A Subversive Way of Thinking

1

Rebelling against the
Rebellion

I think of myself as a New Yorker since I've lived more of my life there than in any other state. But after moving south several years ago, I've tried hard to blend into my new home in Tennessee, which has a rich history all its own—including this interesting little fact I recently discovered from the Civil War era.

Tennessee, you probably know, is shaped like a long, thin parallelogram, which can effectively be drawn into what the Chamber of Commerce calls its three "Grand Divisions"— West, Middle, and East—three equally sized regions that share the same statehood but not always the same politics and perspectives. During the slavery and states' rights debates of the mid-1800s, for example, both West and Middle Tennessee increasingly sided with the separatist sentiments of the Confederacy. Angry at what they saw as the overreaching intrusion of the federal government into their private, personal affairs, they were open to the argument that the only way to preserve their rights and independence was to make a clean break from the established order. Declare their disloyalties. Stand in rebellion.

East Tennesseans, on the other hand, with their mountainous terrain that depended less on farming and agriculture (and, therefore, depended less on the slave labor such livelihoods relied on) remained predominantly allied with the abolitionist Union. Though living in the midst of a southern state bordering on breakaway, the people in the East were not in agreement with the beliefs and practices espoused by the loudest voices who lived in other parts of the state. The city of Shelbyville was even eventually nicknamed "Little Boston." So when Tennessee officially became the last of the southern states to secede from the United States following Lincoln's attack on Fort Sumter in 1861, it did so without the full support of its fellow citizens from the East. Right after Tennessee seceded from the Union, East Tennessee seceded from Tennessee.

East Tennessee was in rebellion against the rebellion.

As a result, they were treated as cross-state enemies, eventually being invaded by the armies and militias of their own state who had been deployed with orders to keep this splinter section under control. They were forced into a sort of guerilla warfare for daring to insist that the rightful rule of their country resided in Washington, DC, not Richmond, Virginia.

In many ways we as believers in Christ—followers of another Ruler, citizens of another kingdom—are much like the people of East Tennessee in Civil War America. We live among a world system that, even though ultimately under the reign of a sovereign God, temporarily exerts a competing authority that seeks to enforce an unjust, unrighteous order on those it claims to rule. The Supreme Court, for example, would later find that the secession of the southern states was an illegal and illegitimate act. Their confederacy had no legal authority. Thus, the United States was always legally sovereign over those states. They just didn't know it.

And so it is with us. The world's illegal rebellion is illegitimate. It certainly *feels* real, of course—IS real—but it doesn't change the reality that God is still Ruler of everything. Though people may *think* they have rebelled, they have not—and cannot—ultimately escape the fact that King Jesus still is sovereign.

And though we feel outnumbered and highly unpopular at times by clinging to our Christian ideals, though we make ourselves subject to all kinds of criticism and misunderstanding by resisting the widely held opinions of our friends and neighbors, we can't help but recognize a tension that keeps us from following where the leader of this rebellion wants to take us. As much as we may feel obligated by our family histories, or as willing as we may be to at least consider the validity of these differing viewpoints, there's no common ground for us to stand on. Our aims are incompatible. As Christians, we don't join an illegitimate rebellion. Instead, we live for King Jesus in contrast to those around us. We live in loyalty to the very One the world rebels against.

We're in rebellion against the rebellion.

So if we know deep down we cannot mingle our convictions with the prevailing moods and modes of the surrounding culture, even out of comfort and convenience, so it seems we're left with only a handful of choices for how to respond to a society in rebellion against our King. We can run and hide to keep from being overtaken, or we can defiantly stand our ground in open, declared warfare.

Or maybe there's a third option. Something less expected, less obvious. More biblical, and amazingly more effective. In a sense we go underground.

Yes, I get that we sometimes want to stay "above ground" as God's people—just attend our churches, have our preferences catered to, and enjoy the ocean cruise while all around us the sea is filled with sinking boats. Yet in a kingdom lifestyle this option doesn't make a whole lot of sense. We've been blessed to be a blessing.

Others, instead, have chosen to live out the gospel and its implications in subversive ways. The reason we can subvert is because the nature of the kingdom is to show first an irresistible social order and then tell about an irresistible king. We go under (sub) where people "out there" don't expect to see and experience grace. We leave our home court (the church) and go to their home court (the world). And then when they least expect it, Jesus shows up in their world, inviting them to draw near to him through our random acts of kindness.

So rather than (or maybe in addition to) inviting the unbeliever to the Sunday morning show, we demonstrate our faith by how we live, relate, and care. Others see that life with Jesus is not about going to a place at 11:00 a.m. on Sunday. Life with Jesus is now demonstrated where they are. The last place they ever thought to look. Right in the middle of where they live, work, and play. We go there.

We stay and subvert.

We can do this another way.

We can become daring agents of God's subversive kingdom.

Prepare to Be Amazed

I would totally understand if this "kingdom" idea has always struck you as being cloudy and mysterious or even if you've never really thought about it all that much. If you have, your tendency may be like many who pocket it away and dismiss the kingdom as a theological concept somehow detached from real life on the ground—lived every day. To many the kingdom is a spiritual idea that makes sense in the context of sermons and Bible studies but not between regular business hours or on Friday nights when you're making plans for the weekend.

And if that's all the kingdom was—a spiritual theme or wordplay that seeks to capture the essence of Christianity in some memorable turn of phrase—we might have the luxury of keeping it at that kind of comfortable, churchy distance.

But the kingdom of God is real.

7

It's here. It's happening.

It's right there in the room with you.

It has broken into our time and space and is subversively working to overcome the darkness of our age. The kingdom of God is a *radical* rejection of every value or point of view that keeps people in bondage to untruth, blinded to Christ's mercy. It is a refusal to classify any person as being expendable or beyond reach, an unwillingness to view any situation as something that cannot be transformed and infused with hope. It means knowing that while not everything will be made perfectly right on this earth or in this era, we have opportunities to witness the kingdom's reality this week on every street, in every neighborhood, and in every nation of the world.

The kingdom of God lives.

Here. Now.

And you and I—undeserving recipients of God's forgiving grace—have been made a part of it. Active participants in it. Agents of change under the rule of our Lord and King, called to join him on a mission that is sure to be victorious in the end. If you are a follower of Jesus, you have been made a citizen of this kingdom.

Because everywhere he leads, his kingdom follows.

But not in ways we might expect.

Subversion in Action

Think of Christ, the conquering King, appearing as a baby in a Bethlehem manger, born in obscurity to humble parents, raised as the son of a poor carpenter in the backwaters of the Roman Empire. Think of his first thirty years spent without unusual notice or public attention, with only one or two events recorded from his early life. Think of forty days spent fasting and praying in a darkened wilderness, quietly and carefully setting the stage for his ministry to begin. Think of his riding into Jerusalem on the back of a borrowed donkey rather than on a royal steed with a phalanx of soldiers by his side.

This is not open warfare. Jesus did not march on Rome. He never called together a zealot army. He never wrote a political manifesto. He simply announced that *because* he had come, the *kingdom* had come—and it would move out from Jerusalem in surprising ways. Not by might but by the subterfuge of lives lived for King Jesus.

And what he visibly displayed through his own unexpected, unconventional emergence into human history, we can now see happening in miniature in our own lives when we—his people, his kingdom agents—act under his orders in the everyday places we're called to serve as ambassadors for this kingdom.

Like Jesus we are enemies of the world's broken system, those who stand against the injustice of a broken world. But as we will see later, the world is ruled (falsely and temporarily) by Satan—yet we live in allegiance to King Jesus. So the way we show our allegiance to God and to his kingdom is primarily under radar and out of sight, composed of small measures that mask their enormous significance. Instead of overwhelming the world with the might of our arsenals and arguments—a "shock and awe" approach designed to undermine the enemy's will or ability to resist—God leads us to a different way of living and thinking.

More creative.

More persuasive.

More subversive.

My wife, for example, recently taught English as a second language to the children of illegal immigrants in our community. Say what you will about the immigration issue—there are plenty of opinions to go around—the fact remains that a sizable number of people from other nations, many of them detached from relationship with Christ, are living in our cities without our having to book travel to Mexico City, San Salvador, or Tegucigalpa to reach them. And it's not hard to see—if you're looking through kingdom eyes—how enabling these kids (and their families) to talk to their peers and communicate within our culture can prove a key, potential connector that leads them into the fellowship of the church and the warm embrace of the kingdom of God.

I know of another woman—in her mid-sixties, with no computer, no e-mail address, and no access to the Internet—who began corresponding as a pen pal with a female prison inmate. Before long, several more of the prisoner's friends were asking this woman to write them. Today she composes longhand letters to more than twenty incarcerated women each month, giving them spiritual guidance, counsel, encouragement, and instruction. Some of her "pen" pals have even stopped by to visit her church upon their release! Here's a lady directly engaging people whose lives have been ruined by falling for the world's way of handling conflict and solving problems, yet she's doing it subversively. Simply. And power-fully. In service to her King and his kingdom.

As I write this, my friend Sérgio Queiroz at Cidade Viva in Brazil is leading his church to write a letter to every pris-oner in their state. After obtaining the list of inmates from the government, he and thousands of others—people under Jesus' rule—are sitting down to tell each prisoner of the grace and love of God through these handwritten epistles.

And that's not all. When I preached at Cidade Viva, it was hard not to notice the prostitutes along the beaches at night—"street walkers" they're often called—half-clothed and looking for a customer. Cidade Viva is taking a rose to each of them—along with an offer of another life—telling them the good news of Christ. Why? They seek to live for the kingdom of God.

The leadership of 12Stone Church, a multicampus con-gregation based in Gwinnett County, Georgia, became increasingly concerned at how home foreclosures, rampant unemployment, and other financial strains were affecting families in the Atlanta area. So they set an ambitious goal of providing relief to five thousand families in their church and community, eventually raising more than $550,000 through designated gifts—many from church members who were themselves unemployed. Partnering with Honeybaked Hams, Kroger grocery stores, and other area sponsors, the church distributed food to each family based on need, culminating with a huge day of giveaways in the parking lot of Coolray Field, home to the Atlanta Braves AAA baseball team. People began lining up hours before the event, jamming traffic flow on nearby I-85, with some of the attendees sleeping overnight in their cars to keep from missing out. "Why are you doing this?" many would ask as they drove by the delivery site, leaving with grateful armfuls of food and supplies.

Because that's just how the kingdom works. Pushing back the darkness and shining the light of God's love into unexpected places is kingdom activity. Drawing people toward the redeeming grace of Jesus Christ and into genuine, saving relationship with him is the kingdom result.

It's subversive. It turns against the way most people think and act—even the religious.

Not sneaky. Not manipulative. Just real and relational, right there in the presence of a broken world.

Like bringing a rose to a prostitute.

And that doesn't fit with how most people, including many Christians, assume the kingdom looks and what it's supposed to do.

Many Christians, if they believe anything about the kingdom at all, think of it as the *church itself,* with its spires and steeples on top that make it almost look like a castle. But while the church is definitely inseparably involved in the work of the kingdom, the kingdom itself is not visible in the same way a church building is. You can't see it with ordinary sight.

That's why lots of people miss it.

John the Baptist, even—the one sent ahead of time to announce the coming of Christ—had a hard time recognizing the kingdom that he himself had said was about to "come near" (Matt. 3:2). Sitting in prison, facing his own execution, having banked his life on the promise that the Messiah was coming to redeem and restore Israel, John dispatched messengers to ask if Jesus was truly the One who was ushering in this kingdom. Perhaps he thought if Jesus was really King of a heaven-sent kingdom, then the one who had announced his appearing shouldn't be locked up in jail!

Jesus' response was to "go and report to John what you hear and see: the blind see, the lame walk, those with skin diseases are healed, the deaf hear, the dead are raised, and the poor are told the good news" (Matt. 11:4–5). Such were the unexpected evidences that "the kingdom of God has come to you" (Matt. 12:28). Jesus was proving himself King over enemies far more destructive and pervasive than Israel's longtime persecutors.

Whatever you thought the kingdom was, John, this is it.

And whatever you think the kingdom is today, I assure you it is more incredible, more surprising, more challenging, and more adventurous than you can even imagine.

It's time for us to see things differently.

To see the kingdom for what it really is.

Jesus and the Kingdom

When I first encountered the biblical message on the kingdom, I was a young believer around fourteen years old, learning to play a worship song on my brand-new guitar. I had never played before, but my youth director saw I had one and asked me to play it at the upcoming retreat—two weeks away. Being eager (at just about everything), I agreed.

"Seek Ye First" uses a simple chord progression—C-G-F, with a couple of variations thrown in there for fun. And I played it again and again, singing the words without really understanding what this song was instructing me to do. I played about the kingdom of God until my fingers bled. But until I read and reread the Gospels, the meaning didn't sink in.

In the years that followed, I was told the kingdom of God was something I didn't need to worry about, that Jesus was going to establish it whenever he comes again. For now the kingdom didn't really matter. I shouldn't be concerned. "That was for another dispensation," they said. But what I could never reconcile with that dismissive attitude was that Jesus seemed absolutely *obsessed* with the kingdom. I mean, read the Gospels. He talks about the kingdom more than eighty times in just over eighty chapters. That's a lot of kingdom. Jesus didn't seem to think we were supposed to ignore it until later.

This is not some minor, unimportant thing. Can't be.

Jesus came into his ministry proclaiming a clear message: "Repent, because the kingdom of heaven has come near!" (Matt. 4:17). Up until that point only a few of his words had been recorded. But with this grand pronouncement he immediately (and repeatedly) began painting a picture of what this kingdom was supposed to look like and entail. Jesus went all over first-century Palestine, the Bible tells us, "teaching in their synagogues, preaching the good news of the kingdom, and healing every disease and sickness among the people" (Matt. 4:23; cf. 9:35).

"Teaching, preaching, healing." Whenever a Spirit-inspired author of Scripture creates a noticeable pattern like this, we do well to look more closely and see what it's really showing us. Through Jesus' *teaching* and *preaching*, he was proclaiming to everyone that they could be part of God's agenda on earth by repenting and believing, that this "kingdom of heaven" was primarily spiritual in nature. And through his miracles of *healing*, he was making visibly evident his authoritative power over the curse of our fallen, helpless condition. After all, "Which is easier: to say to the paralytic, 'Your sins are forgiven,' or to say, 'Get up, pick up your mat and walk'?" (Mark 2:9). They're *both* easy when your power as King is supreme over every part of the rebellious world, both physical and spiritual.

This was how God's kingdom was coming in.

And that's not what the Jews of his day had in mind. They had always expected their long-prophesied Messiah to come and create a restored national Israel that would crush the heads of their enemies. They looked for One who would literally, and at that time, "reign on the throne of David and over his kingdom, to establish and sustain it with justice and righteousness from now on and forever" (Isa. 9:7; cf. 16:5; Jer. 23:5; 33:17)—a political and military king, sent here to set up God's permanent, visible kingdom in a triumphant Jerusalem.

But Jesus' message and mission demonstrated something else—a surprising, subversive kingdom that expanded far beyond this limited and limiting concept. He instead invited people to experience freedom through the forgiveness of sin, not the restoration of civil government. His was an invasion of hope not housed in geopolitical territories but within the human heart, a jurisdiction more infested with hostile enemies than even the Roman-occupied land of Israel. His kingdom wouldn't be marked by armies, generals, and a big palace in Jerusalem. It would be an unexpected demonstration of spiritual power.

So this was not a kingdom they could march into as conquering heroes. They could only be part of this victorious invasion by humbling themselves like little children. Why? "For the kingdom of God belongs to such as these" (Mark 10:14), then as well as now. Richard Lovelace summarizes, "The most crucial battle for the kingdom is won every time a human being repents, believes, and submits to the lordship of the Messiah, becoming a new center for the reordering of life on earth as it is in heaven."[1]

That's why when Jesus was asked questions by the one-dimensional Pharisees, who wanted his explanation on "when the kingdom of God will come," he tantalizingly answered them, "The kingdom of God is not coming with something observable; no one will say, 'Look here!' or 'There!' For you see, the kingdom of God is among you" (Luke 17:21).

Because *Jesus* was among them.

This was shocking news. The Pharisees knew that God was King. They knew he had always ruled the universe from his throne in the heavens. Like Hezekiah prayed in 2 Kings 19:15, they would have declared, "Lord God of Israel who is enthroned above the cherubim, You are God—You alone—of all the kingdoms of the earth. You made the heavens and the earth." That's pretty clear. God is the King of everything—already. They just wanted the earthly kingdom to be made evident.

And yet the kingdom of God was here because the King was here. And that's not what they expected.

God's kingdom was among them, taking over what their *true* enemy (not just Israel's national enemies) had sought to steal. And because Christ our King is within us today, his kingdom remains present among the people in our culture as well. We exist for his kingdom to take subversive shape through our lives.

Saved for Subversion

In 2010 the world watched for a day and a half as thirty-three Chilean miners were brought to the surface of the earth, having spent sixty-nine days trapped a half-mile underground. More than 700 million tons of rock had shifted around their work space, and even those who were charged with the job of extracting them labored for weeks without knowing if any survivors would be found at all.

The progress of their final rescue was accompanied on television by mini-biographies of each individual, as well as live video feeds that captured the anxious anticipation of loved ones waiting topside to be reunited with their brave husbands, fathers, brothers, and friends. Finally the last man was lifted from the rocky depths—another recipient of a new chance at life after what had seemed for desperate weeks a certain death.

Rescued!

"Rescued" is one of the metaphors used in the Bible to describe how God delivers his children from death to life, from the power of worldly rule into the light of Christ's kingdom.

> He has rescued us from the domain of darkness and transferred us into the kingdom of the Son He loves. We have redemption, the forgiveness of sins. (Col. 1:13–14)

The Bible explains that Satan influences mankind to do evil (Eph. 2:2) and enslaves those who follow his will (Rom. 6:16)—the true source behind all those who oppose God and his kingdom (Exod. 1:15–22; Matt. 2:13–18)—and works all day every day to undermine the effectiveness of God's Word (Matt. 13:19) and to blind the eyes of unbelievers so they cannot see the truth (2 Cor. 4:4). This is the condition we were each born into—an oppressive, deceptive kingdom that kept us buried in lies, spiritual laziness, and pointless activities disguised to look meaningful.

But Jesus subversively came into the world to destroy Satan and his schemes, to set free those who suffered under his enslaving rule. Through his death Jesus took on himself both the debt and condemnation of sin (Col. 2:14) and won ultimate victory over the one who uses fear, hopelessness, deception, and guilt as a way to control people's minds and hearts.

We've been "rescued."

Our citizenship has been "transferred."

These ideas are critical for us in understanding the work of Christ and the kingdom. We did not make the kingdom; we were rescued for it and transferred into it.

That word *transferred* refers to the removal of people from one place of residence to another, repositioned for the purpose of forming a new colony. Paul's use of that word in describing salvation implies that we have not only been transferred into Christ's kingdom but also commissioned to be a part of outposts of that kingdom wherever God leads us to go, subversively undermining the tyranny of the evil one.

Don't lose the drama of this. Don't underestimate what the gift of salvation has won for you. Don't downplay the implications of what this calls you to do and be. *Your loyalties have changed from one kingdom to another.* You have been relocated from the haunts of this world's broken neighborhoods, cultures, and systems and have become a citizen of the kingdom of God—all while still living at the same address. If you name Christ the King, if you have been born again by the power of the gospel, if you believe in the sacrifice of Jesus for your sins, your "citizenship is in heaven" (Phil. 3:20).

And that means something.

Special. Radical. Transforming.

Not just a new Sunday schedule but life as a new creation.

Not just a new Bible but a new lifestyle to match.

Not just a new label but a new loyalty.

When I was a kid growing up on Long Island outside of New York City, my dad built us a tree house. An *awesome* tree house. It had plumbing, electricity, cable. (Not really, but I do remember thinking it had everything. It was really cool.) I was eight years old or so, and as kids are likely to do, my friends and I decided this tree house was adequate reason for organizing our own club. So we set up some rules to determine who could be in the club and who couldn't. No girls, of course. Nobody else, either, if we didn't like them. And one more thing: if you wanted to be in our club, you couldn't be in anybody else's. Access to the tree house came with a loyalty oath. You were one of us, or you were left out. Don't try to be playing both sides.

There's no tree house rule in the kingdom, but it sure seems like some people have forgotten that joining this new kingdom (or, in this case, being *brought into* it) requires some radical differences in your loyalties. If a kid with a tree house understands that, so should we. Being a part of the kingdom means a new loyalty to King Jesus.

Something is wrong when churches are filled with people who seemingly haven't changed their loyalties. People who have a religious veneer but live like everybody else. People whose goals and values are little more than "baptized" versions of the world's goals and values. People whose citizenship has been supernaturally transferred into the kingdom of God but who choose not to live like loyal subjects of the King. People who have been rescued from the death trap of the world's domain. But for what? To sit around in church and think they're doing God a big favor by being there? To have the same basic take on everyday life as the people they work with and live around?

Not if they knew whose kingdom they were in, what it cost to put them there, and what it means to be an agent at his command.

One of the most familiar yet radical statements in Scripture comes from the prayer Jesus taught his disciples to pray: "Your kingdom come. Your will be done on earth as it is in heaven" (Matt. 6:10). We're never going to see this culmination perfectly fulfilled, of course, until Christ returns in full glory, when he will bring a highly visual end to the rebellion of the world's system. But until that time our rescued condition—our new kingdom citizenship with its transferred loyalties—compels us into becoming agents of "rebellion against the rebellion," working intentionally to subvert the devil's claim to authority over our and others' individual lives. In a sense we are a worldwide network of underground operatives, poking more holes in Satan's enterprise than he can possibly plug. We live out a daring mission, serving others and pulling them back from his traps while his back is turned on other problems and projects.

Come on. Don't you want a piece of that?

Now, I get that some people will object to this language, and some may take it out of context. I can see it now on some blog site run by a guy who lives in his mother's basement: "Stetzer calls for subversive agents of world conquest." No, the subversive action to which I refer is sharing and showing the good news of Jesus. That's really subversive! King Jesus will come back, and "the kingdoms of this world" will become "the kingdoms of our Lord, and of his Christ" (Rev. 11:15 KJV). In the meantime we are just doing what Jesus did—announcing the good news and living out its message in incredibly subversive ways.

Being a kingdom agent means becoming one who "loses his life" from a worldly point of view (Mark 8:35) in order to find true life for ourselves and to help rescue others who are chained in darkness, doubt, and cleverly disguised despair. It means representing God through his body on earth—the church—as he uses us to advance and expand his kingdom through Spirit-led, subversive ways. It means pursuing a different agenda and mission in life because we serve a different King, living out his teachings as flesh-and-blood realities, not just chapter-and-verse references. When the world zigs, we zag. We give death and its depressing companions (like poverty, pain, and pointlessness) something to worry about.

One simple, kingdom act at a time.

And all the while, Christ claims small, subversive victories in people's lives right around us, in confident anticipation of the day when he will claim every victory there is to claim.

Let's Do It

This book is my attempt to put a face on a vital, biblical concept that has too often failed to congeal in our minds and seemed too unearthly to get our arms around. It took a while for me to get it myself. I'm still just now "getting it" in many ways. But I have never gotten over realizing that God has called me—called *each* of us—to be an agent of subversion in his gospel insurgency. Much of the mystery surrounding what it means to "seek first the kingdom" (Matt. 6:33) has become clear to me as I've seen how God uses our humble submission to his lordship and our faithful participation in the ministry of his church to advance his subversive invasion on earth.

Yes, the kingdom is easy to miss. Jesus' own disciples missed it, in fact, even while staring their King straight in the face. Right up until he ascended to heaven following his death and resurrection, they were still asking, "Lord, are You restoring the kingdom to Israel at this time?" (Acts 1:6). They wanted to know, *Is this the end? Have the end times come?* Still today many others ask the same thing. Yet Jesus puts us on a different path for a different purpose.

So we're in good company to be wondering what all of this means. But we're also in for the adventure of a lifetime if we will assume our places in "rebellion against the rebellion," following our King into whatever subversive activity he wants us to undertake.

2

Secrets of the Kingdom

If not for a good mystery, there sure wouldn't be as many beach-reads to enjoy and no Saturday afternoon matinees at the neighborhood theater to get us out of yardwork. Life would lose some of its exhilaration and intrigue, not to mention those shared experiences around the lunch table the next week, comparing notes with one another about what caught us the most by surprise in this book or in that movie.

But when it comes to real life, we like to keep our mysteries to a minimum. We like to know which way the interest rates are going, what's causing that groaning noise under the hood, whether we should be concerned about a phantom pain in our side, why a friend seems to be acting differently toward us than usual. We want to know. We need information.

No mysteries.

Throughout the early part of Jesus' ministry, he used some extensive teaching and healing episodes to give hints at what his kingdom looked, felt, and sounded like—slowly unraveling the mysteries, inviting others to enter into it. He even started showing how some of those regarded as religious leaders were actually opposing the work of God's kingdom by their narrow self-righteousness and the control they attempted to force on people from their respective theological camps.

Then came Matthew 13. A seismic shift in Jesus' teaching method. His kingdom mysteries were about to become a whole lot clearer.

But not to everyone.

That's because Jesus didn't spell out the kingdom in dictionary definitions. Although Jesus was almost obsessed with the kingdom (with dozens of references and teachings about the kingdom in the gospels), he never broke open the dictionary or encyclopedia and read out, "Here is how I define the kingdom." That's frustrating sometimes to people like us, but Jesus had a reason for not giving the definition, time, and place.

Everyone would have been expecting that. He instead gave real-world *descriptions* of it by means of *parables*, word pictures drawn from everyday life that were so vivid and relatable, they seized the hearers' attention and stirred up questions in their minds about what the metaphor could mean. Made them think, not just sip from a spoon. He intended these parables to *guide* them into an understanding of the kingdom (the way the best learning always occurs), not just *tell* them.

But here's the best part: since his parables were so perfectly crafted—yielding just enough spiritual information to pique interest but not so much to get bogged down in needless minutiae—they were able to resonate in receptive, inquisitive hearts while simultaneously clanking off the ears of those who were predisposed to being hardened to God's truth anyway.

So, yes, they were mysteries. Riddles. But only to those who really didn't care to know them or (more important) be governed by them, to reorient their thinking around them. We know this because Jesus came right out and told his disciples:

> The secrets of the kingdom of heaven have been given for you to know, but it has not been given to them. For whoever has, more will be given to him, and he will have more than enough. But whoever does not have, even what he has will be taken away from him. For this reason I speak to them in parables, because looking they do not see, and hearing they do not listen or understand. (Matt. 13:11–13)

That's subversive. Jesus was saying that the kingdom is happening right out there in front of everybody, but if you're not looking for it, not interested in it, not inclined to be changed by it—no matter how amazing it is—then you won't be able to see it. So it was with me for a long time. Maybe it's true for you.

This verse relates not only to unbelievers (who simply do not possess the necessary wiring for being attuned to God's Spirit; see 1 Cor. 2:14) but also to those believers who are too much in love with their religion to be a part of the King's work, those who are more invested in their church and its Christian subculture than in the steady invasion of Christ's influence on the world around them. To these people the parables of Jesus may seem like nice, sweet stories but not subversive secrets.

If, on the other hand, you are ready for your radical rescue and transfer into the kingdom of God to change your whole way of viewing life—everything from church and family to career and finances, from vacations and Christmas to shopping and Little League—these secrets are put right in your lap to explore and experience. They're yours. Take 'em. Run with 'em.

They're only secrets because not everybody knows them.

But *you do*. Or at least *you can*.

And this chapter is where we meet up with some amazing ones.

Seed

"Consider the sower who went out to sow" (Matt. 13:3). Jesus' first parable speaks less about what the kingdom *is* than how the kingdom *begins*.

It begins with a seed.

This is the same "seed" Peter was talking about when he said we've been "born again—not of perishable seed but of imperishable—through the living and enduring word of God" (1 Pet. 1:23). It's what the psalmist was referring to in saying that "though one goes along weeping, carrying the bag of seed, he will surely come back with shouts of joy, carrying his sheaves" (Ps. 126:6).

The *seed* is the Word.

The Word starts everything—"the word about the kingdom" (Matt. 13:19). This is what God uses to produce an exponentially expanding realm of his rule and influence, "some 100, some 60, and some 30 times what was sown" (v. 8).

No Word, no kingdom.

Each of us has been raised on certain givens, standards, and traditions that may or may not find their basis in scriptural truth. The ideas that motivate us, determine our priorities, frame our ethics, and inform our behaviors can come from anywhere—books, interviews, random trails of thought that float into our ears and bounce around in our heads. But only the Word can produce kingdom fruit. If our lives don't start there, they cannot lead to anything that eternally matters.

Jesus taught a striking message about this Word—that is, a kingdom-sprouting seed, producing fruit only in receptive soil.

So our first job as subversive kingdom agents is to be people who "receive the implanted word" (James 1:21). This doesn't mean the Bible is the only thing we can ever read, but it does mean our impact on this culture and generation—both as individuals and through the church—depends not upon our skills and timing or our grasp of certain business models. It doesn't even depend on our eagerness to know, our sincerity to learn, or our desire to experience the Word. It depends on our willingness to receive humbly and in faith the message of the gospel. That's what the kingdom looks like.

We must resist being merely familiar with this Word and drink it as if our life depends on it (1 Pet. 2:2), letting it change our whole perspective and expectation of life. God's Spirit will produce an explosion of kingdom growth *within* us, then (better yet) *through* us.

We already know what happens when our hearts are beaten hard and resistant to God's Word. We know what it's like to give him little room for squeezing seed between the tiny cracks in our schedules. We know when our soil is so full of other interests and concerns, there's not much daylight left for the small shoots of spiritual possibility to take hold and actually do anything. In other words, *we have all been the path, the rocky ground, and the thorny patch before.*

But, for those who are in the kingdom of Christ, we've received the Word with receptive ears and have seen the truth with spiritual sight. We've experienced the fruit of the kingdom.

When we face hard times, our soil often dries up and hard soil forms. Or when we get busy and distracted, our Christian life begins to gasp and sputter from lack of nutrition. We produce fewer kingdom fruits.

But when our hearts are truly receptive to God's Word— letting it live, grow, and germinate in us—our Lord will take care of making things happen in the fertile soil. Our desires and attitudes will become *his* desires and attitudes. Things will start sprouting from our work and testimony we never thought in a million years we'd see attached to us. The people around us will be changed and challenged by what just naturally comes up in our conversation—not occasionally but regularly and consistently, in surprising amounts.

Because when the seed strikes root in good soil, the new life that springs up is a living, breathing, flesh-and-blood agent of his subversive kingdom. And with that kind of structure underneath us, we can go out intentionally with great determination to undermine the evil world order and set free its captives—especially as we join together with other believers in the church who are feasting on the Word themselves. That's how God creates entire fields of bumper kingdom crops, both here in our communities and around the world.

The Word that changes us is what also changes others.

Justin Holcomb is a man whose love for the Word has set the agenda for his life. His father was lying on the beach in 1973 when someone shared a single seed of God's Word with him. As a result, this trackless hippie left behind his lifestyle in the commune, married Justin's mother (a month before he was born), and raised his young son in the church with a steady dose of seed being poured into his heart.

By 2001, Justin's ministry heart had increasingly drawn him toward the ravaged plight of the southern Sudanese, an impoverished people who have practically lost an entire generation to widespread civil war and the cruel, oppressive hand of their government to the north. Further exploitation has come from a group called the Lord's Resistance Army, a renegade patrol force notorious for child abductions, sexual assaults, and physical mutilation of their opponents. Yet a rebel movement has sprouted up—the Sudan People's Liberation Army—to defend their land from governmentally endorsed barbarism. And Justin has been traveling to this African region each year to teach SPLA chaplains the Word of God.

Such trips frequently find him teaching the Bible amid the snap of AK-47s firing in the background, while all around him lies the physical carnage of war and the heartbreak of preventable diseases. But through the motivating power of the Word, Justin and his wife, Lindsey, have used their presence in Sudan to meet the health and lifestyle challenges of a culture stripped of its resilience and resources. Their nonprofit organization, Mosaic, gives away thousands of mosquito nets each year, offers training in both literacy and tailoring skills, provides a home for girls whose families have sold them into the sex trade, and supports area pastors in southern Sudan and neighboring Uganda.

That's what a seed can do.

Change a man. Change a family. Change a life. Change a nation.

What might it start growing in you?

Weeds

So Jesus' first parable dealt with how the kingdom of God *begins*. The second reveals how it *develops*.

Get ready. It's not pretty. It might discourage you, but it's important that it informs you. These are important issues here about how we understand the kingdom.

Jesus said the kingdom of God is like a farmer who sows wheat (sows the "seed") in his field (Matt. 13:24–30). But while he's sleeping, his enemy sneaks in and scatters weeds in the same field plot. For a little while, no one can tell what's happened. But when everything starts coming up, the workers look around and see unwanted growth in the seedbeds. The field is a mix of wheat and weeds.

The first thing they do is go to the farmer. Has he seen what's happened? Who could have done this? What does he want us to do about it now? Go out and pull those weeds up?

The farmer, seemingly unrattled by the problem, tells his men just to let the weeds grow right alongside the good crops, fearing that in trying to extract the unwanted growth they might yank up some of the healthy young wheat by mistake. But at harvest time, he says, when everything's ready for cutting, they'll separate everything on the threshing floor, storing the wheat away in the barn and bundling up the weeds for burning.

That'll take care of that.

But that's for later.

For now, Jesus was saying, even though the kingdom of God is definitely establishing a presence in enemy territory, ours are not the only footprints on the farm. By no means have the opposing forces surrendered. And believe it or not, the Messiah didn't come to eradicate their presence from the earth right away.

Well, you can imagine this parable certainly didn't sit well with those who expected God's coming kingdom to be a sledgehammer of total domination in Israel. Truth be told, it's not exactly what we like to hear either. This particular secret of the kingdom is one of the big reasons why our job here as Christians is so much harder than we sometimes think it ought it be. If it weren't for all these weeds around—blocking our sunlight, cramping our style, acting like they own the garden God created—life would be a whole lot simpler, wouldn't it?

But that's not reality, not according to God's sovereign design for kingdom life on this fallen planet. Wheat grows with weeds. That's just the way it is.

But there's one other secret we can learn from this parable of Jesus that ought to give us at least a little relief. For even though our lives must be shared with people who don't like what we stand for and would prefer they had the whole place to themselves, *we are not responsible for weeding.*

You've gotta like the sound of that.

Look, we will never take over this world for Jesus. Let that sink in for a moment. I've read the end of the book—King Jesus wins. But it is not you or I that usher in the victory. Our role is not to bring in the kingdom. We can't. It's not in our job description or part of our performance review. Yes, the day will come when the enemy's little weed-producing operation will be put permanently out of business, but it will be Jesus who does it—not us—and he won't need our help to clamp on the padlocks. The idea that all of our efforts can eventually win enough turf battles with the world's system to usher in Christ's kingdom on earth is not what we see in Scripture. And learning to manage our expectations around this reality is an important key to healthy kingdom subversion. Only God can usher in his final and completed kingdom.

In fact, to think any other way can be spiritually problematic. If we think it is our job (and within our ability) to take over the world, then we often act that way. When Christians start trying to moralize the unconverted from positions of power so that the "nation will be just," they end up hindering the mission rather than advancing it. They think this tactic will make the world as King Jesus wants it to be, but they have missed the message that this is a spiritual kingdom until Jesus makes it an earthly one.

Some people love the perceived opinions and politics of King Jesus more than they love the King himself. Yet Jesus never promoted his politics, although he did respond to political questions. His kingdom is so much bigger and better than a slogan, picket sign, or bumper sticker. His kingdom involves people living revolutionary lives. In fact, from producing a coin in the mouth of a fish to pay his taxes (Matt. 17:27) to one of his most famous governmental policy-related responses— "Give back to Caesar the things that are Caesar's, and to God the things that are God's" (Mark 12:17)—Jesus seemed to continually resist political subversion. Political subversion polarizes kingdom citizens from the mission of the King. We are passionately in love with the King and his kingdom. The kingdom is all about the King and nothing about our agendas and opinions as his citizens.

By the end of the New Testament, the early church had established a beachhead in most of the major cities of the Mediterranean region. But its presence was small in comparison to the overall population. In fact, the powers that be viewed the church as merely a sect within Judaism. So these fledgling bands of believers chugged along under radar until the second century, growing quickly but quietly, remaining subversive as they wormed their way through the enemy's spiritual strongholds.

Then in the second and third centuries, two great plagues swept through the Roman Empire, wiping out entire cities and causing people literally to run for the hills, escaping to more rural areas where they could hopefully avoid being caught by the epidemics. One group, however—the Christians—stayed behind in large numbers to care for the sick and poor and hurting and dying in the established cities. This visible, selfless demonstration of compassion radically changed the culture's understanding of the church.

People became followers of Christ in droves. Soon the majority of those living in the Roman Empire had converted to Christianity. Even the emperor himself claimed to have become a Christian. And not only did he *legalize* Christianity in the realm but eventually *required* it of every citizen. Rome became what was soon called a "Christian empire"—sort of.

It looked like they'd uprooted all the weeds.

But whenever the church starts basing its moves and mentalities on worldly patterns of power and influence rather than the "seed" teachings of God's Word, you can be sure the weeds will start spreading like wildfire. That's precisely how the powerful, healing, liberating church of the first and second centuries degenerated into just another business-as-usual religious institution.

It lost its subversiveness.

Wheat without weeds just doesn't happen. Never has. Never will. Not until Jesus comes back to deal with weeds the way only he can. So for now we ought not be surprised to see the telltale weeds of enemy presence in our cities and workplaces, in our families and neighborhoods, in our government and nation. Everywhere. That doesn't mean we're losing the battle. It just means we're experiencing subversive kingdom life, which isn't always neat and tidy and finished up in time to go to bed at night. It doesn't continually give off the appearance of victory. Not every day. Not even on most days.

But that's OK. Because we're not here to weed. Our job as subversive kingdom agents is just to keep sowing and tending the wheat, keep pouring ourselves and his Word into the people's lives around us—teaching, helping, serving, ministering, pushing back the darkness by our presence, faithfully manning our work while waiting for our God to come back.

Don't worry about the weeds.

Just keep growing more wheat.

Start Small

We tend to think big is good, and bigger is better. When something is big—a church, a business, a movie, a movement—good things must be going on. Size is a sure sign of success.

I've spoken at dozens of the largest churches in America—several with more than ten thousand in attendance. These churches have all the marks that make people think they are successful. Yet ironically, the best of those megachurches are not fooled by their own size. They know that the small interaction of disciples, lives, and groups is what makes their life together matter.

But that's what makes the kingdom of God so baffling and backward-sounding to most people. Successful kingdom activity doesn't have to come with brisk retail sales, a snazzy logo, celebrity endorsements, and a marketing campaign. It doesn't have to generate ten million user hits or get written up in *Newsweek*. In fact, it's often just the opposite. Kingdom work is typically most recognizable by how small it is.

The kingdom is like a mustard seed, Jesus said (Matt. 13:31–32). You seen one? You may keep a little jar of them in your spice rack at home. They're tiny. They're nondescript.

In our *Subversive Kingdom* small-group curriculum that accompanies this book, we shot video about this (and the other parables). We brought along some mustard seeds to illustrate the point of the small seed. My job was to hold them so all could see. The only problem? The seeds were too small. So in the video I held a handful to make the point—that's small.

The kingdom is also like yeast (v. 33)—another household item that hides behind the much larger items on your pantry shelf. A person who didn't know any better would think it was just some sort of dust or powder. Nothing special. Probably unnecessary.

But something significant is happening here with mustard seeds and yeast. And whatever it is, it's not going to stay small for long.

As agents of transformation in God's subversive kingdom, we don't have to apologize for being few in number, focusing on one little area or need around us, making what seems to be a small impact. Our King's own teaching tells us not to be thrown off or discouraged by worldly perspectives that minimize what we're doing or try to stop us from getting started altogether, making us perceive our kingdom work as being too insignificant to matter.

Small strides are actually God's deliberate design for effective growth. It's how his kingdom happens. Jesus was born in a manger in a little town on the backside of nowhere, and today more than a billion people on the planet consider themselves his followers. That's kingdom economy. A mustard seed "becomes a tree, so that the birds of the sky come and nest in its branches" (v. 32). Little by little it produces shocking, unexpected growth until "birds of every kind will nest under it"— representing all the nations of the world—"taking shelter in the shade of its branches" (Ezek. 17:23).

Eric Geiger, until recently at Christ Fellowship Church in Miami (and now my colleague at LifeWay), explained this verse in the context of their church. God has blessed their growth to more than seven thousand people each week. They have resources and reach beyond most churches. They've become a "tree, so that the birds of the sky come and nest in its branches" (Matt. 13:32). They seek to serve the community so that others might "take shelter" in the ministries of the church. Each small group, for example, is challenged to participate in mission projects designed to serve the community. They believe the communities surrounding each campus should benefit from the church's presence in that particular context.

That's subversive. That's a turn back against the flow of culture in both the religious and irreligious sectors. Christ Fellowship is not focused merely on getting the city of Miami to attend their church (although no one would argue if they did). Christ Fellowship is obsessed with getting the people of their church into the city. That's counterintuitive to even we church people who have reduced the mission of God to Sunday morning attendance.

Again, this doesn't mean the kingdom is going to overtake the enemy completely during this age. The time when Christ will visibly rule "from sea to sea and from the Euphrates to the ends of the earth" (Ps. 72:8) is awaiting the chosen moment of his return when all will look around and know that "the kingdom of the world has become the kingdom of our Lord and of His Messiah, and He will reign forever and ever!" (Rev. 11:15).

But for now we plant seeds.

We watch them grow.

We subversively permeate a culture that only seems able to judge big things by how big they currently appear. They would never guess that at this moment the lives and activities of kingdom agents like you and me are working "like yeast that a woman took and mixed into 50 pounds of flour until it spread through all of it" (Matt. 13:33). The word for "mixed" here could also be translated "hidden." Yeast is *hidden* in bread dough. Once it's in there, you can't sort it back out. It's already made its subversive impact. It's already started turning a lump into a loaf. How's that for transformation?

That's what we and our churches are intended to do—not to stay in our Christian closets but to get out and mix with the confused society around us, sowing seeds through our gospel message and our acts of Christian mercy. Just as yeast can do no good for the flour if it's never pulled out of the jar, isolated believers do little of kingdom benefit if they keep themselves removed from a culture held captive to the evil one.

Your church (and mine) does not exist to keep us away from the world. Parables like this remind us of that. Yet we each experience a lot of energy pulling us the other way—to stay away from "those people" and only be with people like us. But that misses the point and ignores the parable. We are to "mix in" not so we might be like the world but that the world might know King Jesus and see his kingdom impact.

This is a kingdom secret of Jesus—one that will either land and take effect in your receptive heart or will blow by you into thin air if you're not honestly wanting to be changed, challenged, and obedient to his truth. Spiritual growth and maturity shouldn't lead us *away* from contact with unbelievers but rather right into the midst of them (see Christ Fellowship). We cannot subvert the kingdom of darkness by lighting nothing other than our own homes and churches. We only succeed as agents of transformation when Jesus "spreads the aroma of the knowledge of Him in every place" (2 Cor. 2:14).

Small things, subversively placed, lead to big things in God's kingdom.

Joy

Few people really experience joy.

Sadly, too many Christians are among them.

There is little joy in simply keeping current with religious rules and obligations. A kingdom citizen has a biblical ethic that matters to him as well as a keen sense of right and wrong in God's eyes. But a typical churchgoer who sees the gospel as merely her or his ticket to heaven, who feels obligated to put money in the offering plate each week, and who wishes they didn't so feel guilty about some of their bad habits is not having much fun. They haven't discovered the incredible joy of living lavishly in the presence of their King. Kingdom citizens do have responsibilities before the King, of course, but these things are not drudgery to perform; they are a response to his love and grace.

Jesus taught this as a crucial principle of kingdom life when he was training the first twelve disciples. We get a rare glimpse into one of his training sessions when he said: "As you go, announce this: 'The kingdom of heaven has come near.' Heal the sick, raise the dead, cleanse those with skin diseases, drive out demons. You have received free of charge; give free of charge" (Matt. 10:7–8). I wonder if the disciples were overwhelmed with the realities of their assignment. Much grace and energy is required when ministering to the marginalized, right?

When exploring Matthew 10, you actually discover many great principles that apply to kingdom life—the kind that lead to joy and adventure, even as we go about our Christian duties and disciplines. Specifically notice the redemptive culture of the kingdom. Kingdom citizens enter the room to bring grace and comfort. They are ambassadors of the King (2 Cor. 5:20), and you can tell they are in the room by what they do. Everything begins with an announcement that connects activity with the King and his kingdom: "the kingdom of heaven is at hand." The question addressed by the announcement is "Who sponsored this event?" Revealing the Sponsor is important for both the speaker and the hearer as a reminder of the ultimate power of the kingdom.

As the King and his kingdom reign, life changes for the better. The typical struggles are no longer struggles. Kingdom citizens don't stop after they "get the word out"; rather, they bind wounds and help the hurting through the power of Jesus. When redemptive, situational care happens, both the giver and the receiver know that the kingdom is happening right before them. Kingdom ministry is not found in words alone or deeds alone but in both word *and* deed.

Another interesting principle is that kingdom citizens minster grace out of grace. Their source of joy and freedom is found here. Caring for hurting people is not about fulfilling obligations or relieving guilt (all of which have already been taken care of by the King). A secret of kingdom life is that citizenship is a gift freely given by the King.

By the way, this is what makes the kingdom so subversive. Few people think, even if there is a God, that he would conduct his affairs without charging handsomely for his services. Historically, religion is about people addressing their innate fears of going to hell or making God angry by giving him plenty of money and time. But in Jesus' kingdom, fear and obligation are replaced with joy and gratitude. So much has been given that the natural (or supernatural) response is to pass it on to others. Kingdom citizens are never more like their King and never represent him better than when they give. Citizens do not have to protect themselves or their assets because the King continually, by his grace, replenishes what he asks citizens to give away. What a great economic plan.

The person who has authentically given his or her heart to Jesus cannot hope to derive all their joy from knowing that his/her own eternal problems are taken care of. That's because the good news is not merely the fact that God has saved *you* but that he can save repentant sinners everywhere, that he sent the Lord Jesus into human history to establish his kingdom and reconcile the world to him. Being part of *that* subversive mission is what gives Christian living its incredible joy. Seeing the kingdom take visible shape in people's lives as a result of your touch, your time, and your simple testimony will leave you too excited to sleep.

Overjoyed.

The kingdom is like the "treasure" a man uncovered in Jesus' parable (Matt. 13:44) that made him want to run out and sell everything he owned in order to make that gold mine part of his own backyard. The same discovery caused a delighted jewel merchant to sell his lifetime collection of merchandise in order to possess this "one priceless pearl" (v. 46).

To *be* in the kingdom is amazing. To *live* for the kingdom is indescribable joy. A joy you can't get enough of.

Occasionally I see joy like that in the faces of my three daughters. When Kristen and I saw a bear in the parking lot of Yosemite or when Kaitlyn first walked into Times Square at night with me. But for Jaclyn it was in our own backyard.

Jaclyn is my middle daughter. She loves horses and she loves adventure. One day not long ago, her passion was directed toward digging for buried treasure in our yard. I've told her, "Look, we don't live on some abandoned pirate island. There's no map out there with an 'X' that marks some spot within our property line." But nothing has deterred her from turning our lawn into a minefield of freshly dug gopher holes.

Especially after she finally hit pay dirt!

"Daddy, Daddy, I found treasure!" Jaclyn came screaming across the lawn one afternoon. No, it wasn't pieces of eight, but I'll admit it was a pretty cool horseshoe, fastened with old, square, metal nails. She found "treasure," and it was from a horse! And with this one find as motivation, the gopher holes have started increasing again. That's because once you find your treasure, it's all you can think about. It's all you want. You want more.

I believe that's where Jesus was going with this kingdom secret. Once we understand the unmatched value of kingdom living, we'll want to pursue it with everything we've got. Instead of following the pattern of pivoting away from the lost, poor, hurting, and needy, insulating ourselves from other people's struggles, we'll go where people need us the most. Instead of finding another gymnastics class to add to our family's already overblown schedule, we'll let the kingdom direct how we orient our children's lives, investing our time and resources into things that reflect Christ's calling. Instead of retiring at sixty-five into self-absorbed inactivity and the fruits of our career labors, we'll consider ourselves redeployed into an army of revolutionaries more interested in collecting kingdom fruit than souvenirs and seashells.

Because that's where joy is found.

So if you and joy haven't been showing up in the same place very often, it's likely because you've been looking for it in things like good food and Sunday football. Or perhaps you've been so busy driving around, dusting furniture, and keeping things from falling apart, there's not much of you left to enjoy anything after a normal day of business and activity.

As sure as God's Word is true, kingdom treasure leads to joy—like nothing else can do. And if you haven't yet located those kingdom experiences for which you'd give up everything else to be part of, ask God to show you where to find them.

They're out there. Just waiting for you.

The joy of every subversive agent on a mission that changes everything.

Secrets Revealed

Yes, the kingdom of God has its secrets. But like everything else about the kingdom, Jesus doesn't deal with these the way most secrets are handled. He doesn't keep them to himself, hushing them into silence to keep from being overheard. Instead, he shares them generously and plentifully—even with his enemies—like seed thrown out by a farmer. They're not secrets because they're hidden; they're secrets because they're a mystery, shrouded to both the world and the disinterested religious, yet able to be grasped by any believer who's truly hungry to hear.

So even though we may say we don't understand the kingdom of God well, we actually know quite a lot about it if we're really listening. The kingdom of God . . .

- is informed and initiated by the Word of God.
- is designed to take place in the midst of the world.
- uses small things to grow big things and impact lives.
- offers a joy that's otherwise unavailable to the human heart.

As simple as all these sound, they are not acceptable to a world that has its own ideas about how things work and what's important in life. These concepts don't square with those whose religious traditions make them more comfortable being exclusionary and off to themselves. They are incompatible with churches that are more focused on growing bigger than they are on being true to their kingdom calling and sensitive to the Spirit's direction. And that's why these mysteries remain walled-off secrets to many.

Maybe one of those people has been you.

Now would be a good time to come honestly before the Lord, confessing that you've let the world's "business as usual" influences infect your mind and determine your ways of operating, that you've allowed a self-centered complacency to dull your spiritual senses and pull you away from what ought to be your number-one thing.

For too many and for too long, we've reduced Christianity to a moralistic philosophy of life—do this, go to church, don't do that. Yet it's so much more. The kingdom of God has broken and is breaking into the world. We have been transferred into it and made to be a part of its work. Yet many are satisfied with steeples and pews and songs to keep us happy, rather than being a part of the work of the kingdom.

Maybe it's just that we have become distracted. Our focus in church has become too much like a carousel, with lights and music that keep us upbeat but ultimately going around in a circle. Life in the kingdom is so much more. Yet many miss out. I've missed out.

I'm reminded of this statement by C. S. Lewis in *The Weight of Glory*:

> We are half-hearted creatures, fooling around with drink and sex and ambition when infinite joy is offered us, like an ignorant child who wants to go on making mud pies in a slum because he cannot imagine what is meant by the offer of a holiday at the sea. We are far too easily pleased.[1]

So it is for us. We are far too easily pleased with religion rather than the reign of God. We are far too pleased with the comforts of the church rather than the work of God's kingdom. And in doing so, we are missing the blessing of being part of something that is so much more than a moralistic philosophy of life.

Lots of us have been there. We all know the feeling. But if you don't want to be looking the other way when God has kingdom plans for you, if you refuse to alter your religious calendar and connections in order to engage with people's true needs in culture, or if you're tired of being more at home in the sinful world than actively subverting it, then come back and be part of an underground movement to overthrow the oppressors of God's lost children.

It's no secret this is where you belong.

3

Already, but Not Yet

June 6, 1944.

D-Day.

The amphibious landing of nearly 160,000 soldiers on the beaches of Normandy, along with twenty-four thousand paratroopers who coasted to land amid foggy darkness and tracer fire, put Allied forces within range of German soil for the first time. After many long months of planning an assault on Nazi batteries, this successful advance along fifty miles of coastline—forged against daunting odds and at the cost of nine thousand lives—dealt a crushing blow to the enemy's hopes. D-Day was the beginning of the end of World War II.

But for almost another full year, the fighting raged on, inflicting more casualties on both sides than any other stretch of the war. Through France. Into Germany. The Battle of the Bulge. Across the Rhine. But knowing their cause was just, knowing how much was at stake, and knowing they had already sealed the war's ultimate outcome with their Normandy invasion the previous summer, the Allies kept pushing forward to the bitter end. To the streets of Berlin.

And finally, on May 7, 1945—a week after Hitler's apparent suicide in the bomb shelter under his chancellery—VE Day! Victory in Europe. The war in Europe was officially over.

On D-Day, the end of the war was *inaugurated*.

On VE Day, the end of the war was *consummated*.

This wartime analogy paints a picture of what kingdom life is like on the time line of history and what kingdom life is like today. The kingdom's inauguration occurred when Jesus appeared on earth in flesh, dealing a subversive "beginning of the end" to the oppressive rule over humanity, an evil tyranny that dates back to the beginning of men and women. When Jesus strode from the tomb a resurrected Savior, his victory over death, hell, and the grave was a done deal.

But the advance and work to establish God's kingdom was far from over. And so from Christ's ascension to this very day—and for as long as we're required to wait until he returns to fully and finally consummate his kingdom—his followers have work to do. We're called to announce how Christ frees those around us from enemy captivity. We're commanded to call men and women to repent and believe the saving news of Jesus Christ—to plant those "seeds" that can bloom not only into new, believing hearts but also into new field agents, recruited for subversive duty in an ongoing gospel insurgency.

Such is life "between the times."

A famous twentieth-century sermon framed the context well by declaring, "It's Friday, but Sunday's Comin'." The message was first well-known in the African-American context. It often spoke of the oppression of the day and the promise of a future that would be different. That's still true today. It's applicable to us all in this broken world.

It does not take much to see that the world is broken and the kingdom is not yet fully realized. But we clearly see that the kingdom is here, now, and real. It's real but not fully realized. It's Friday, but Sunday is coming.

These are the bookends of God's kingdom calendar. In a sense we live between the Good Friday of kingdom conquest and the Easter Sunday of kingdom coronation. And so, where does that leave us—followers of Christ wanting to fulfill our mission in the "already, but not yet" experience of everyday life?

It means, as Philip Yancey writes, "It's Saturday on planet Earth."[1]

And this Saturday is a workday.

Caught in Between

Look around. Our world is broken. I'm not talking about the "world" in terms of nature (although creation, too, bears the marks of sin's blemish and decay). I'm talking about the "world" comprised of the people, structures, and systems that make up society—the moral patterns, beliefs, and behaviors that result in things like unfair business practices, racism, extreme poverty, dishonest government, dirty politics, family breakdown, cheating, stealing, oppression of the weak, and so many other distressors and defilers.

In this world people who possess an evil thirst for power are often able to get it. People who harbor selfish desires can usually find a way to succeed at manipulating and taking advantage of others. People who feed on human weaknesses and depravations have little trouble exploiting those who can't (or won't) control their lusts.

Head gaskets blow. Jobs are deleted. Friends get sick. People die.

You see it everywhere you look—the unjust normals of earthly life. Damp, dirty blankets trail out from under cardboard boxes beneath a city bridge. Retirement savings plummet in value just as their account holders need to tap into them. Trees go down in a thunderstorm, making the homeowner's premiums go up. Punk burglars break into a person's house, and all the police can do is file a meaningless report.

It stinks.

It's bad.

It's not right.

It's broken.

And in homes and hospitals every day of the week, at courthouses and gravesides everywhere in the world, people of all spiritual makes and models suffer from it—from a world that toils along in hopeless disrepair.

What many of these people probably don't know, however,

is that the only place where all of this turmoil will be made right—all sickness, anger, discord, and broken relationships; all birth defects, hunger, addictions, and bankruptcy—is in the eternal kingdom of God, to be evidenced one day in the unchallenged reign of Jesus Christ. Only in him will any of us experience the ultimate destruction of impurity, disease, sadness, and loss; of hurricanes, tornadoes, tsunamis, and floods. All of it.

Because this kingdom (though not yet *consummated*) has already been *inaugurated* by the appearing of Christ on earth, we and the church have a meaningful role within the "already, but not yet," in-between time we call this present time. More than having a role, we sense inside us a God-given *desire* to alleviate as much pain as possible with the tools and opportunities he has placed at our disposal. We hate watching people suffer from the debilitating effects of evil in the world. We want to see the fallen and broken world, with its hurt and pain, driven back and overthrown. We may be pretty good at drowning out our heart's compassion with large doses of television and ice cream, but deep down we want to be part of making a difference in others' lives.

That's because we not only have what many have called a "God-shaped hole" in our hearts that he alone is able to fill; we followers of Christ also have a *kingdom*-shaped hole that makes us want to be part of what God is doing on this earth.

Trust me. I know.

I was raised in a messed-up family. My father was an alcoholic (now recovering), and as a result our home was the site of a lot of anger, aggression, and dysfunction. Growing up in that kind of environment gives a person a deep-seated yearning to escape and find something better. To be something more and to do things differently become a life mission and sometimes an unhealthy obsession when you are an adult child. When you see messed-up for what it truly is, you know you want out of it—to do whatever you can do to change it. But when I trusted Christ as a teenager, I became eager for something else—something more than just imagining a way to make my own life easier to deal with. I wanted to be a soldier in God's subversive kingdom, to get swept up in a great battle to thwart the forces of darkness and shine his light into other people's lives. Like many of the other Christians around me, I wanted to find out what seeing the kingdom unleashed could do to fix things around here.

Even if you're not like me—even if you come from a place of stability, warmth, and nurture—you are aware that we're living in a messed-up world. This place just ain't right. And it's not getting any better. But as a believer in Christ, you know your Lord came as a suffering Savior. You know that all history is rolling toward a colossal sum-up when evil will be destroyed and God will rule from his undisputed throne. And so with totally assured confidence that you *cannot fail* in an ultimate sense, you can feel turned loose to take on your subversive calling in a serious way. You can unite with others in your church to put the world on notice by living God's Word together in the midst of hurting, seeking, unhealthy humanity.

You see, by living and engaging in this way, you know that you cannot ultimately fix everything. That is God's job. Jesus will return to do that. Yet now, right here, I can live faithfully, doing kingdom work—not to fix everything but to do something that King Jesus would lead me to do.

This, by the way, is why the church itself should not be theologically equated with the kingdom of God. Jesus came announcing the kingdom, and the church emerged as a result. So rather than the church's being an institution that pushes God's kingdom agenda, the kingdom is what gives birth to the church, then God himself advances his kingdom agenda through the life, work, and ministry of his people.

As big as the church is, the kingdom is even bigger.

So in this sovereignly ordained meantime, we have an obligation to represent what the kingdom of God looks like, as seen in stark contrast to the world around us. Compelled by a vision of Christ's coming rule—when relationships will be restored, races reconciled, differences settled, and injustices made right—we launch into a campaign to subvert the world's temporary hold on our attitudes and experiences. We live out God's kingdom through our lifestyle, and we demonstrate his kingdom through our ministry and service.

The kingdom is already, and we announce the "not yet" as we live toward its coming—as we work for the kingdom and as we wait for the consummation of that very kingdom.

That's what we're here for.

Here, "in between."

In Business

Jesus was near Jerusalem when he told those around him a parable, not many hours before he would ride into the city amid shouts of deceptive hosannas. It started like this: "A certain nobleman went into a far country to receive for himself a kingdom and to return. So he called ten of his servants, delivered to them ten minas, and said to them, 'Do business till I come'" (Luke 19:12–13 NKJV).

No coincidence that Jerusalem was near. Jesus' disciples were still certain he would one day be ruling from this great city on his messianic throne. But his word to them was of a king who had ventured away, leaving his subjects to take care of business until the king's return. *This was a kingdom secret.* And that means it's something for us to understand as well if our hearts are open.

Kingdom life "in between" the time of the king's departure and his return is populated by believers in Christ who function as subversive agents of his kingdom. To believe otherwise is to be caught simply *existing* as Christians, so focused on the promise of a kingdom we'll one day inherit, we don't feel responsibility for engaging in the mission that's already in front of us. Worse yet, when blinded by this haze of inertia, we usually find ourselves more susceptible to being shaped by the world around us than by God's Word and his truth. We lose our compelling reasons for resisting the pull of culture's self-interested standards, and we forfeit the opportunity to make a present-day kingdom difference the way God has commanded us to do.

This can't go on.

Not if we're going to be the subversive agents we've been sent here to be in the "already, but not yet."

Later in this book, in the part where we'll examine more

closely our "Subversive Plan of Action," I'll be dealing in greater detail with the strategies such a mission entails. But for now let's summarize it like this, in three points, seeing them in conjunction with the kingdom secrets we've already discussed.

1. Our mission is to share Jesus with a broken world. Not everyone sees this as a primary or central point. Some think the only means of expressing the kingdom is by performing good deeds—caring for the hurting, correcting injustices, handing out help and relief. And listen, I am all *for* the church doing these things with abandon! That's a big part of what this book is about. Jesus explained the subversive nature of his mission when he said: "For even the Son of Man did not come to be served, but to serve, and to give His life—a ransom for many" (Mark 10:45). Notice how his mission turned against religious and political culture. For the religious, a king would be served and given extravagant gifts (see Bethlehem). Political leadership would be delivered through power and manipulation. Now we both serve and give pointing to the ultimate sacrifice of our King. The message and messenger collide with a cultural view of leadership. The kingdom is not about winning but about rescuing.

But while this part of our mission is extremely important and is (admittedly) too often overlooked and deemphasized in many Christian circles—to our shame—we lose our distinctive calling if by ministering to others' visible needs we downplay the gospel that inspires it. The kingdom begins with the "seed." That's why in some of their final words with Jesus before his ascension, when the disciples asked what was going to become of his kingdom, he said the Holy Spirit would soon descend upon them, "and you will be My witnesses in Jerusalem, in all Judea and Samaria, and to the ends of the earth" (Acts 1:8). To make "disciples of all nations" (Matt. 28:19) is why we've been left here. This is our kingdom mandate.

2. Our mission includes alleviating the needs around us. Again, this follows closely on the heels of the first point; the two are nearly inseparable. Both should be happening so seamlessly in our lives and in the work of our churches that you can't tell one without the other. For as surely as people are lost without Christ, they are also hungry, thirsty, estranged, naked, sick, and in prison (Matt. 25:42–43); and our Lord commands us to care for them. I mean, he himself defined his ministry as being focused on the poor, the captive, the blind, the oppressed (Luke 4:18). So, therefore, we join him on mission not only when we proclaim his saving gospel but when we confront injustice, when we touch human need, when we seek to bring about changes that transform this world to look more like it will be when Jesus returns. The "not yet" aspect of life means the "weeds" of pain, abuse, worry, and danger are next-door neighbors with God's people. But because we are also subversive kingdom agents, we go underground to help others experience his concern in the here and now.

Jesus ties them together so clearly in what is often called the Great Commission. He says, "All authority has been given to Me in heaven and on earth. Go, therefore, and make disciples of all nations, baptizing them in the name of the Father and of the Son and of the Holy Spirit, teaching them to observe everything I have commanded you. And remember, I am with you always, to the end of the age" (Matt. 28:18–20).

So he tells us to make disciples. This involves, at its core, sharing Christ. Then he says to "teach them to observe everything I have commanded you," which includes doing what Jesus said—like feed the hungry, visit those in prison, and so much more.

3. Our mission focuses on both the local community and the larger world. I'm so glad to see the rising concern among churches for unreached people groups, peoples around the world like the Dhanuk of India who have not yet heard the gospel. Spiritual lostness and oppression abound to the far corners of the earth, and we must pursue our kingdom mission to the uttermost parts with great passion and determination.

In addition, that kingdom activity often starts small, and oftentimes we are called to pursue our kingdom mission in overlooked places—in our own neighborhoods. For some of us, our kingdom mission opportunities begin first in our own communities in addition to partnering with others in the nations of the world. It may not be as exciting and exotic to subvert our own hometown needs with the power of the gospel, but this mission that takes us everywhere means it must also take us right here—right where we live—as ambassadors of a consummated kingdom to our own cities and communities. Then we can (and do) partner with others around the globe on a kingdom mission there.

As a young church planter in Buffalo, New York, I got to know another pastor there who served in our urban area and became a good friend to me. The social problems that existed around us were extreme to the point of being oppressive and unsolvable. Liquor and porn shops were everywhere. Crack use was epidemic. Human destruction was bought and sold in broad daylight. And our best attempts at infusing hope and transformation into that kind of city dynamic often felt like mopping the rocks around Niagara Falls. Pretty pointless.

But this was where we lived. This was the flashing neon "not yet" where God had called us to minister, share our faith, and try reaching people for Jesus. And while we did our work as faithfully and energetically as we could, my pastor friend took it to a bold extreme, publicly and loudly protesting to counteract the many evils that kept our community drunk, addicted, and mindlessly depressed.

The inner city of Buffalo was not a happy place to be. Like most other inner cities, people in Buffalo were marginalized by poverty, homelessness, and addictions of all sorts. Yet for me, I focused on sharing Christ to the exclusion of everything else. I was planting a church and did not want to be distracted by all those social activities.

I asked my pastor friend one day why he was spending so much time working against the liquor stores and porn shops. He frequently went to government meetings, pushed issues of zoning, and tried to limit their influence. He was still very much involved in sharing the gospel and pastoring his church, of course, but he still made time for these other activities. He wanted to make the community more like God intended it to be—a better reflection of the kingdom of God. While I prayed on Sunday, "Thy kingdom come, thy will be done, on earth as it is in heaven," he was (on Monday) working toward making the world more as God desired it to be.

His reply taught me something valuable about being an agent of God's subversive kingdom. "Ed," he told me, "we both spend our ministering here, dragging dead and dying people out of the river to save them. I just think it's OK to go upstream and tell the people who are throwing them in to stop it!"

Here's a guy who was fully aware how sick and broken the world was. You didn't have to walk twenty yards in any direction to see that. But instead of being beaten into hopelessness by the often ugly "not yet," and instead of waiting coolly for a heavenly kingdom existing somewhere out there on the horizon, he set both feet inside the dark reality around him and sought to subvert it. Knowing how the kingdom looks, he worked to bring its light into the grungy bars and back rooms where evil and brokenness were thought to have exclusive run of the place.

He challenged me that I, too, needed to act as an agent of God's mission. Agents of transformation don't sit back, unconcerned with the world and its pain. Their desire is that the world would look more like the kingdom they're called to represent until the people living and dying inside it are shown the way to live forever. They care about their community and the world, and they work for social justice in all places.

Already.

Look Who's Coming

We *know* this. And we *want* this. We want to be *part* of this. But sometimes with all the weight we carry in life, with the often difficult task of serving an invisible God in a visibly broken world—not to mention the discouragement of our own faults and failures that keep hanging around and dragging us away from deeper intimacy with Christ—we need help in stopping to remember something:

God's coming kingdom is awesome.

And it is unstoppable.

Remembering what God is holding in reserve for his people is absolutely imperative if we want to stay on track and on mission with our earthly purpose.

Some people perceive our present reality as some sort of cosmic conflict between good and evil, as if some lingering doubt remains as to which side will ultimately win. But don't let anybody tell you differently. Our King's victory is totally assured, and the day is coming "when He hands over the kingdom to God the Father, when He abolishes all authority and power," when he "puts all His enemies under His feet"—including death, "the last enemy to be abolished" (1 Cor. 15:24–26). The whole of our broken world will be fixed. Everything within the theater of God's creation will be restored. Life on earth will be delivered from bondage, liberated to be the way it was supposed to be "in the beginning."

That's what is coming. That's the secret reality we live knowing. And that's what we are here to declare and demonstrate to our world while we wait for this kingdom to finally arrive.

Peter says it will happen like this:

The Day of the Lord will come like a thief; on that day the heavens will pass away with a loud noise, the elements will burn and the works on it will be disclosed. (2 Pet. 3:10)

Notice he doesn't say the *earth* will be destroyed but rather the "works on it will be disclosed"—or "burned up," to cite some of the older translations. Peter in this passage had just mentioned Noah's flood (vv. 6–7), a judgment of God designed to wipe wickedness from the face of the earth—an event with which Peter's audience was certainly familiar. Using the flood, Peter points to the future judgment of God—purging enemies of the kingdom from the earth. This next cataclysm, however, is going to be different, he said. Tullian Tchividjian explains:

> The wicked things that are "swept away" by water can grow back (as happened in Noah's time). But the wicked things burned up by fire can *never* come back. The burning-away effect of fire is permanent; the sweeping-away effect of water isn't. Fire, in this case, is better than flood.[2]

When God sends his purifying fire to purge the earth of corruption, everything will be "disclosed" for what it is. Sin, immorality, deception, and death—all of them will be laid bare as thieves of God's glory, liars in regard to his goodness. Unlike the temporary pushbacks against wickedness, disease, suffering, and poverty that have occurred throughout history or in other situations closer to our time and space, this one will be complete. Permanent. Always. Evil will be banished from the earth. The king of darkness will be "thrown into the lake of fire and sulfur" to be "tormented day and night forever and ever" (Rev. 20:10).

No longer, then, will we need to be agents of kingdom insurrection. No longer will weeds grow up around us in the seedbed. Our King will reign with his people, and the earth will be totally redeemed from the whole sinful order. God's revolution will be complete. His creation will have come back to him full circle.

And everything that happens next will be new to our experience, to those who've been saved through the blood of Christ Jesus.

New Jerusalem. Israel in the Old Testament was meant to draw all nations streaming into Jerusalem, where everyone could give praise to the one true God. When Israel rejected her calling, however, as well as her revealed Messiah, God scattered his people into the world to share the gospel outside the former boundaries. But when Jesus returns to consummate his kingdom, his unified people will all gather again in one place to dwell forever and ever—a new city for the people of God, a new home for redeemed humanity. Wow.

A new temple. The Old Testament temple had been designed to help people relate to God's presence on earth. In the New Testament we're told that our own bodies are now "a sanctuary of the Holy Spirit" (1 Cor. 6:19), meaning that we ourselves are empowered to represent him to the world. But John, looking around near the end of his revelation, could find no grand temple in New Jerusalem. And here's why: "The Lord God the Almighty and the Lamb are its sanctuary" (Rev. 21:22). In Christ's consummated kingdom we will never be without the visible presence of our King. Imagine that.

A new life. We've read about it and heard it preached for years. But don't let the rolling eyes of earthly cynicism dilute it into fairy tale for you. There is a "not yet" attached to the new life you've received and are currently experiencing in Christ. And this life described in Scripture is beyond our imagination:

> Then I saw a new heaven and a new earth, for the first heaven and the first earth had passed away, and the sea no longer existed. I also saw the Holy City, new Jerusalem, coming down out of heaven from God, prepared like a bride adorned for her husband. Then I heard a loud voice from the throne: "Look! God's dwelling is with humanity, and He will live with them. They will be His people, and God Himself will be with them and be their God. He will wipe away every tear from their eyes. Death will no longer exist; grief, crying, and pain will exist no longer, because the previous things have passed away." (Rev. 21:1–4)

A new kingdom is in the future of kingdom citizens. No more fractured relationships to manage or feel wounded by. No more terrorist threats or tainted food recalls. No more thoughts of death to keep us up at night. How *could* there be, since there won't be any more "night" to experience— absolutely nothing to make us think back on a life that was so regularly troubled by fear, anger, bitterness, anxiety, and lingering doubts? They're all gone. All the time.

Keep all of this in mind.

Read about it and meditate on it often.

Remember the "not yet" reality we are here to model and live.

Because, yes, the current state of life on this planet sure has a lot of brokenness. You're right to be dissatisfied with it. But it's not enough for Christians merely to recognize that the world isn't what it ought to be and that people are suffering in ways they shouldn't have to suffer. Our sorrow and indignation must lead us into subversive battle so that God's freedom and justice can be experienced here. "On earth as it is in heaven."

Glimmers of his new creation.

Renovate

The rest of this book is my attempt to flesh out what these kingdom realities should mean both in our personal lives and in our shared life together with other believers in the church. How should this "already, but not yet" experience of ours affect our choices, relationships, and objectives? What does our hope and confidence in God's kingdom inspire us to be and to do?

The answer is as exciting as it is exhausting. I'm not going to kid you.

There's no sugarcoating to subversiveness. It's contrary to the values of the world around us.

Paul, writing in Romans 8, says that all creation "eagerly waits" for the day when it will be "set free from the bondage of corruption into the glorious freedom of God's children" (vv. 19, 21). In other words, God's gracious plan of redemption for his people is the model for what he will one day accomplish on earth by restoring the original purpose of his created order. So we (the church) not only represent the first taste of this transformation to the world—simply by our saved presence and the changes God is continually bringing about in our lives—but he is also putting us to work repairing what is broken in the people and environments around us.

We're on his renovation crew.

And that's good. Good and hard.

Years ago at our inner-city church in Buffalo, we bought a building that was more than a hundred years old, formerly the meeting site for a Brethren of Christ congregation. It was in bad shape and needed a lot of work, starting with the shocking discovery that the walls had been insulated with nothing but newspaper. In the wall we could read original accounts of the 1898 sinking of the USS *Maine* in Cuba's Havana Harbor. It was fun to find, but it also revealed the reality that this restoration project was going to be a lot more difficult than we thought. Renovation projects always are.

And it never changed. We would fix one thing only to uncover another problem. After fixing that one, two more would crop up. Soon we came to the same conclusion anyone involved in a major renovation project eventually realizes—there's always more broken than you think.

And that's what we can expect as renovators of a broken world. Regardless of what God leads us to tackle, the needs and issues before us will be greater than our ability to meet them. We'll be tempted to think it's useless even to try sometimes, since so much is working against us and the problems are so stubbornly thick with history and complexity.

But as believers who carry inside us an "already, but not yet" mentality, we possess what it takes to focus on more than just the immensity of the restoration. Hope, faith, and perspective encourage us to swing the hammer at whatever is in front of us that day, at that moment. And by faithfully doing what we can, showing and sharing the love of Christ as we go, the subversive work of each day is worth its own reward.

It doesn't fix everything, but it's valuable just the same. It may not fix the whole world, but what a difference it can make to the widow or the orphan.

The Old Testament judge Shamgar is an illustration of this. He doesn't get the same kind of biblical press as more famous judges like Deborah and Samson do, which likely means his leadership and exploits on Israel's behalf were not marked by miracles as theirs were. But when Philistine patrols were threatening his people, Shamgar picked up an oxgoad and took down six hundred of his enemies (Judg. 3:31). He started where he was (probably at his farm—where *else* would you have an oxgoad?), used what he had, and did what he could to deliver Israel from oppression, at least for that day. That's one day more.

Gary Haugen, founder of the International Justice Mission, is a present-day example of the same thing. When he began his outreach to free the victims of exploitation and other forms of sexual and violent oppression in our day, he might have considered the job too big to wade into had he been able to visualize the twenty-seven million men, women, and children who are currently being held in slavery worldwide. But "while the kingdom of God will be complete only in the coming of Christ," he says, "today our great joy and privilege is to work as colaborers with the Creator in extending his kingdom over one more life, one more family, one more neighborhood, one more community."[3] Gary knows he can't fix it all, but he can help rescue one little girl trafficked from the Laotian highlands. To her it means the world, even though the world is still broken.

So don't be surprised at how much more broken you find the world than you even realized it was when you began.

Start where you are.

Use what you have.

Do what you can.

And don't be afraid. The kingdom that's already been inaugurated is on its way to being consummated. And though the size and scope of the renovation is more than we can get our arms around, we have reason to be heartened rather than disheartened because we're not expected to fix everything. The full repair won't be ready for revealing until Jesus returns to establish his kingdom completely. But in the meantime his work of restoration gives us a calling to undertake and a reason for getting our hands dirty.

So get ready to get subversive, rebels.

It's worth the hard work.

And just wait till you see how it's going to turn out in the end.

PART II

A Subversive Way of Life

4

Becoming Your Kingdom Self

Every once in a while, some offbeat religious zealot will point to historical patterns on his charts and graphs, flag them with random bits of Scripture, and declare with prophetic certainty that the return of Christ is sure to occur on one specific calendar day. Insight that had long been overlooked and foolishly misunderstood by others is now as plain as day in the eyes of this anointed storehouse of spiritual knowledge. In fact, he and his followers are said to be already in the process of liquidating their worldly effects and preparing for a grand rendezvous with Jesus on, say, the fifth of March or something. Can't miss. Not this time.

Media outlets—knowing that a quirky, end-times tease is sure to keep their audiences hooked through a couple of commercial breaks—go national with the story as well as a brief summary of its odd mathematical rationales. Interviews with the gullible adherents appear in newspapers and on the morning shows. *Doonesbury* creates a weeklong series of strips satirizing the coming event. Late-night TV hosts lampoon it with one-liners.

Harold Camping predicted the end of the world on May 21, 2011. He had done it before, but this particular prediction caught the world's attention. I was not really impressed so I took to my Twitter account and announced, "Harold Camping, please apologize and use familyradio.com to tell your now-broke followers what they should do." Well, the tweet went viral, ended up in *USA Today*, in newspapers in India and Australia, and everywhere else. It reminded me—watch what you tweet.

Yet for many of us, after much hype and publicity—most of it tongue-in-cheek—the "magic day" rolls around. On that day people with little reason for taking these silly pronouncements of nutty Christians too seriously go to work and run their errands; they keep their dinner plans in place; they stop for gas on the way home; they go about their normal routine. But perhaps at some point throughout the day (if most of them are being genuinely honest), the possibility does at least cross their minds: What if this guy is right? What if today's the day? I mean, it *could* be.

Makes you think.

Would you consider yourself ready to meet God this afternoon or before bed tonight? What kind of impact would the gravity of that revelation make on your plans for the day?

Even if you only knew that Christ was returning at some time in the next five years or so, how would this knowledge alter your activities in the meanwhile? How much busier would you be for Jesus if you knew he was that close to coming back?

Ask a few colonial Americans of the late eighteenth century.

Around noontime on a spring morning known to history as the New England Dark Day (May 19, 1780), the sun became virtually obscured in the sky, everywhere from Maine to New Hampshire, down into Massachusetts and Connecticut, even as far south as New Jersey, where George Washington reportedly mentioned the fact in his diary while on Revolutionary War duty. (The story is in Wikipedia, so you know it's true!) The night birds began to sing; flowers closed their petals; cattle in the field displayed unusual behaviors. For a period of time that extended into the following day, the entire northeast region was shrouded in an eerie darkness.

Scientists from the University of Missouri School of Natural Resources have since studied tree rings in the area that indicate this strange phenomenon was likely the result of Canadian wildfires, belching smoke into the upper atmosphere. But for New Englanders on the ground in 1780, with no CNN to consult for explanations, they filled in the blanks with their own assumptions. To this day, devout Seventh-Day Adventists consider it a sign of biblical prophecy when the skies went dark that day.

Most people were sure it was Judgment Day.

According to historical accounts from the Connecticut legislature, the gathered representatives debated whether they should continue meeting or go home to face the end with their families. Even if the fearful, unpopular decision was made to stay, they would be forced to bring candles into the assembly hall in order to conduct their business, even in midday. They couldn't see to conduct business.

The scene among these government officials was understandably unsettling. Some panicked. For sure, many prayed.

Some probably began trying to cut last-second spiritual deals with a Deity they only knew by name if not by relationship.

But then with calm courage, a state politician of whom little else is known to us through historical records rose to his feet and said in everyone's hearing (if John Greenleaf Whittier's poem "Andrew Davenport" is as accurate as it seems):

> This well may be
> The Day of Judgment which the world awaits;
> But be it so or not, I only know
> My present duty and my Lord's command
> To occupy till He come. So at the post
> Where He hast set me in His providence,
> I choose, for one, to meet Him face to face,
> No faithless servant frightened from my task,
> But ready when the Lord of the harvest calls;
> And therefore, with all reverence, I would say,
> Let God do His work, we will see to ours.
> Bring in the candles.[1]

"We're working here—bring in the candles."

That's the kind of confident posture you and I can actually live in as believers—being ready at a moment's notice for Christ's return—not feeling the need to fear the results of his appearing or to try cramming a lifetime of neglected work into the short time we have left. Having placed ourselves within the steady, ongoing flow of his kingdom activity— whatever he has called us to do—we can live "waiting ready" between these first and second appearances of our King.

Wouldn't that feel good and strong?

That's how I want to live—and I am guessing how you want to live. To live in the confidence that we are doing what King Jesus wants us to do—what he left us here to do. So when he "shows up," we are not "in trouble," but we are ready.

But too many believers in this "already, but not yet" season of history do not see for themselves a kingdom mission and ministry in which to actively engage. They don't practice a life that's actually under the Spirit's control, both in matters of personal conduct and in actionable priorities. That's why I often refer to this period of time as the "missing middle"— because the church is largely not fulfilling the role it is called to play in this hour. By not feeling compelled to live as subversive agents of transformation, substituting it instead with either organizational routines or worldly complacence, we are not (in the words of James Davidson Hunter) being "faithfully present" in the world.[2]

God says, "It is already the hour for you to wake up from sleep," to shake off the stupor that blinds your motivation for being dedicated to purity and committed to kingdom service, to "discard the deeds of darkness and put on the armor of light" (Rom. 13:11–12). As the Lord gives the direction and equipping, you and I are to stay focused on the shared task before us.

But what does this ask of us personally? What kind of people is he calling us to be? How are we supposed to approach this subversive task so we prove faithful, confident, and effective while waiting for his sure return?

The answer, as always, resides in what Jesus said.

Life in the Middle

Matthew 25 is packed with intriguing kingdom parables and analogies that help us understand what life is supposed to entail for us in the "missing middle," or the time between the first and second coming of Christ. The first of these parables depicts in living color the attitude I've already been talking about so much in this book—the watchful, confident waiting that is expected of those who are looking for the "groom" to appear (v. 1), for him to "consummate" his kingdom. The ten virgins who had trimmed their lamps with oil, certain of being in place when he arrived, stand in obvious contrast to those caught scrambling to make themselves ready, those trying to play both sides of the spiritual fence, hoping they end up in the right place at the right time. As followers of Christ and seekers of his kingdom, we are called to be consistently alert because we "don't know either the day or the hour" when our Lord will come back to establish his consummated reign (v. 13).

Jesus' next parable, however—the parable of the talents—adds a second element to this season of expectation; and that's what I want talk about in this chapter. Our lives are to be marked not only by *prepared* waiting but also by *active* waiting. It's not just *waiting* that matters; it's waiting *ready*.

You remember the story. We've already looked at it briefly. A wealthy man goes away on a trip, leaving his servants in charge of his estate. But instead of just telling them to sit tight and wait for him to show up again at some point of his choosing in the future, the master graciously entrusts his own possessions to them and (according to a parallel account in Luke 19) charges them to use their various stewardships to "engage in business until I come back" (v. 13).

Which, unbeknownst to them, is going to be a while.

This is huge.

When Jesus told this parable two thousand years ago, most of his hearers probably weren't even able to grasp the details of what he was talking about. They likely didn't realize that *he* would be the one going away, that *he* would be the one not coming back until after he'd been gone "a long time" (v. 19). And yet even after Jesus' eventual death, resurrection, and ascension—even when his followers began putting the hopeful pieces of this parable together as they thought back to it or heard it retold in various settings—they could never have imagined that "a long time" would mean more than their own lifetimes. They certainly could not have believed, not in their wildest dreams, that some generation of mankind would still be living here on planet Earth two thousand years later, still carrying around their God-given talents, still looking up occasionally to see if the silhouette of their master was approaching on the horizon.

But this call to "engage in business" is what gives muscle and meaning to our Christian lives and to the fleshing out of our kingdom selves. We are not just waiting for the fulfillment *of* the kingdom; we are called to take active, responsible roles *within* the kingdom—for as long as we're here, for as long as it takes—even till our deaths if that's what happens first before the time is ripe for his return.

So we live today between verses 18 and 19 of Matthew 25, between the distribution of kingdom responsibility and the settlement of kingdom accountability.

Living between the times waiting for the King to return is a strange place to be. Yet we know the feeling. For some it's one of dread. Growing up, I did a lot of dumb things when my parents were not home—and dreaded their return. Yet there were times when I was ready (admittedly, fewer times than when I was not). In those cases I was not just ready but happy to have them return because I was doing what they had asked.

And here's what we learn from those who first played this role in Jesus' kingdom parable. The following three points contain the heart and attitude we must strive to embrace if we are going to be useful agents of gospel change.

1. Be his. The device Jesus used in this story to illustrate the principle of responsibility was the *talent*, a unit of currency quickly recognizable within his culture. So we're certainly not reading anything foreign into the parable if we say it speaks to how we should handle money as kingdom citizens. But we can equally say that the applications of this story are not *limited* to money. Truth is, God has given us *many* things to manage with an eye toward being agents of transformation in the world. He has given us *actual talents*, for example—human skills and abilities. He has given us *time* to invest in his kingdom activity. He has given us *energy* to expend in strategizing, coordinating, and implementing various kingdom initiatives, or just in keeping an open awareness for Spirit-inspired moments throughout the average day when we can push back the darkness and brokenness in the lives of those around us.

But no matter which of these directions we want to take in applying this parable to our lives, the primary point is that the "talent" Jesus talked about was the *possession of the master* (v. 14). Whether giftings or opportunities or physical resources or whatever, everything we own belongs to God. We are his. There is no way to be an active, responsible kingdom agent without getting that, knowing that, and living that.

The things in your possession today have been "entrusted" to you (v. 14 NASB), not sold to you, not deeded over into your name. They're not yours to assign for other purposes or to decide you don't want to use them anymore. Your assets are visible testimonies—living proof—that your Lord has work for you to do for his purposes and his glory.

So by choosing to engage with him in what he wants done through your life, you must make a bold act of surrender, resisting the urge to garner credit for yourself or to outdo other people by comparison, while also refusing to squander your available resources on yourself or your own agendas.

But this is not as much of a sacrifice as it sounds, for in getting busy with kingdom opportunities, you are assured of a lot of things that make this God-centered state of mind worthwhile. You will enjoy, for example, the purest rewards of hard work. You will know the incomparable feeling of God's "well done" (vv. 21, 23). You will experience a refreshing freedom from bitterness and hurt feelings. You won't care anymore about not being recognized as the one who got something started or made things happen. By humbly, deliberately remembering that God has given you these possessions for the advancement of his own plan and fame, you can spend a lot more of your days in steady confidence than in guilt, emptiness, hesitation, or regret.

Because being fully God's is a good thing.

It will keep you from hoarding stingy control over your money when God nudges you to share with someone else. It will keep you from being paralyzed by insecurity in exercising a skill you know you possess but have always been afraid to risk exposing. It will keep you from making cookie-cutter decisions on what to do with a Sunday afternoon or a week of vacation and maybe turn it into a service activity that changes someone's life while simultaneously changing a lot about your own life as well. It will keep you from being that one-talent guy who stashed his treasure in a hole in the ground, afraid he'd just make a mess if he ever tried doing anything with it. That's actually the fruit of worrying about self instead of living with sold-out ownership to God.

In the end all these "talents" with which we've been entrusted will be handed back over to the One they truly belong to. And for everything he's entrusted to us that we've used for his glory, his kingdom, and his purpose, we'll be amazed that we're returning even more to him than we received in the first place. Like the first two servants in Jesus' parable, we will see in our open hands that he has blessed our God-centered work—like he always does—with his multiplying power. Be his!

2. Be different. Not only did the "talents" in Jesus' parable belong to the master, they were also his to apportion at his own choosing. And as he distributed them individually to each of his servants, he didn't give everyone the same amount. That's just how he decided to do it . . . the same way God still does it today.

And that doesn't always seem fair.

But that's because we've been trained by this world to believe that everyone deserves an equal shot at everything. We think if we're all on the same footing before God (as we are), then we shouldn't have to operate with less ability, wealth, finances, intelligence, or good looks than other people do.

Look around, though, and the truth is plain to see. We are not the same. By God's design. Some people seem to be good at everything—comfortable speaking in public, quick with a good joke, skilled with their hands, blessed with a solo-quality singing voice. Then here *we* are, all thumbs and elbows, apparently expected to be as effective in the kingdom as everyone else, only without all the tools God has opted to give others.

This is a great spiritual challenge for many. We're not always pleased with how God has made us. We wish we were somebody else. We feel pressured to be something we're not. Even the few strengths or abilities we do possess don't often seem like the ones worth having, or at least they're not always valued highly by the people we're around and whose opinions matter most to us.

I don't mind telling you I struggled with this a long time. My dad was a union iron lather by day and a backyard athlete by night and on the weekends. He wanted me to be a natural-born ballplayer just like him, and he worked hard to mold me into his image. In an effort to make sure I got started on the right foot, he signed me up young for baseball and even volunteered as the coach. I was his worst player. It was humiliating to him, I am sure, but it was mortifying to me.

Pitching, hitting, and running bases just weren't my thing. They weren't my "talents." I preferred instead to sit in my room and read the encyclopedias. One year I read the entire World Book set, A to Z, all the way through. Is that weird or what? I knew, of course, this wasn't what most kids my age wanted to do with their afternoons and evenings. It certainly wasn't who my dad wanted his son to be. I was sensitive to how different I was and unsure what to do about it. For many years I had difficulty squaring these unusual interests of mine with a world that ascribed status and acceptability to things I hadn't been given—things I couldn't have done well even if I'd wanted to. Later I realized God blessed me with how he wired me, but it took some time.

You see, as kingdom agents, we must be able to come to the place where we thank God for who he's made us to be and what he's given us to work with, as different as it may be from everyone else. I'm not talking about quoting some syrupy self-worth mantra about how special we are and how good it feels to be me. I'm talking about recognizing that God has shown great purpose in creating and redeeming us a certain way—a way that fits precisely into his sovereign plan for our lives. For not only has he drawn up a mission for us to complete, he has bestowed upon us everything required to accomplish it. And if we fail to agree with his wisdom in doing so, we will not be able to return to him the profit he rightfully expects from what he's given us. We'll miss what we were placed here on earth to do.

In reality each of us, even with our differences, has been entrusted with great resources and responsibilities. Not little, but much. The "talents" the master handed out to his servants were each large monetary sums. Even the man who received only *one* talent was in possession of a small fortune since this single measure of currency was perhaps as much as twenty times the annual wages for a servant of that day.

So seize what you've been given—whatever it is—as a declared treasure from God. Embrace and employ it with the confidence of one who knows that his Commander would never send him into battle ill equipped and destined for failure. It's not just OK to be different; it's your kingdom calling to be different. And by living out what God has given you—however little it may seem—you prove his just-right equipping to be amazingly larger than life.

3. Be faithful. We make a lot of promises, but we don't always make a lot of progress. We get started on things we don't typically finish. We do more gearing up than wrapping up. We're more want-to than follow-through. We turn over new leaves but don't leave behind many trees.

We are not always faithful.

And this is simply not an option for those who seek to live their lives for God's kingdom mission.

If you were expecting Christian life to come with light requirements and easy exemptions—if you thought any old excuse would be blithely met by God with a wave of the hand and free hall-pass permission—you've bought a line of religious thinking that is all beach and no sunburn. You're looking at kingdom living not from a foxhole but from a fun park.

God calls us to faithfulness.

The master in Jesus' parable meant business when he came back and "settled accounts" with his servants (Matt. 25:19). The only way to "share" in his "joy" was for him to hear that they had used well what he had given them (vv. 21, 23). In a hundred different terms and tones of voice, up and down the pages of the Bible, Scripture calls each of us to be "good managers of the varied grace of God" (1 Pet. 4:10).

To be faithful.

Every believer has been designed by God to bring him glory by serving his kingdom agenda. Each one of us has been given a part in his grand scheme to subvert the broken system of the world. We have been individually handed our five-, two-, and one-talent assignments and led into battle with the full resources of heaven at both our front and our flank. Our one job now is just to jump in there and do it. Work it. Give it. Mean it.

Too often our kingdom activity is gapped around our

entertainment schedule. We intend to turn our attention to it, but right now just isn't really the best time for us. We start to say something or do something out of obedience to our kingdom mission, but the situation seems to call for a delay. Keep this up long enough, however, and our delays can turn into a decade—the lethargy into a lifetime. Waiting to serve him faithfully until we have a little more control over our schedule, until our finances are in better shape, until our life circumstances start to stabilize—that's hardly subversive; it's just convenient. And under no conditions is it good enough.

Notice what was said to the servant who ran off and hid his talent in the ground, failing to put his gift to good use for the master: "You evil, lazy slave! . . . Take the talent from him and give it to the one who has 10 talents. For to everyone who has, more will be given, and he will have more than enough. But from the one who does not have, even what he has will be taken from him" (Matt. 25:26, 28–29).

This is no little matter. God is no pushover grand-parent. He gives no breezy, accommodating allowances for his servants' inaction. He is a Lord and Master who expects his assigned mission to be all encompassing enough that we get up and go places with it—at great cost to us, yes, but also at great reward. For to the ones who proved themselves faithful in Jesus' parable, the master was equally quick to say, "Well done, good and faithful slave! You were faithful over a few things; I will put you in charge of many things" (vv. 21, 23). Didn't matter if they'd started out with two talents or five talents, ten or twenty, one or a hundred. All that mattered was this: *they were faithful.*

Never forget that the God who *entrusts* is also the God who *expects*—not so he can be hard and taskmastering toward us but rather to give us ongoing work that yields joy and purpose and confidence and value. His assignments lead us to a newfound freedom in worship and a genuine desire to see those trapped in the world system liberated by Christ's love and compassion. Some would call this kind of accountability narrow, overbearing, and recreationally restrictive. The kingdom agent calls it the kind of life that lets him experience the unhindered flow of God's blessing.

See if any other life can do that.

Irreconcilable Differences

To sit around idly waiting for Jesus to come back is neither biblical nor subversive. It's not kingdom focused and, frankly, not very compelling. The Christian life is so much more than many Christians live it. They're redeemed, so they figure they can just rest until his return. For too many and for too long, we've made it acceptable to sit there week after week and do nothing and still call yourself a Christian. But if a Christian is not one who is transferred into Christ's kingdom to live as the King's agent, I am confused. The Scriptures teach us that we are "reconciled" to be agents of "reconciliation" (2 Cor. 5:18).

We've got work to do, not our own, but led and empowered by the Spirit.

It's interesting that this exhortation comes amid one of Paul's two letters to the Corinthian church because we know from what we read just how irreconcilable the Corinthians' lifestyles were with God. They were selfish, full of evil and corruption. Were the kingdom to advance there, a wicked culture stood to be drastically changed and leave an indelible mark. But to do so, the Corinthians—just as today's kingdom agents—needed to deploy with an awareness of three critical perspectives.

First, kingdom agents must remember that *at a point in time they lived lives as irreconcilable as any Corinthian they could ever meet.* The phrase "living like a Corinthian" was commonly used to describe anyone who lived out of control sexually. We were all Corinthians before Christ saved us. We were all living irreconcilable, out-of-control lives on some level. We all remain Corinthians in recovery from something. But God, through his great love and grace, has invited us to a new life into the kingdom that has changed everything. Now our message is one of love and testimony of God's grace. "Old things have passed away" (2 Cor. 5:17) for us Corinthians.

So ask yourself: *Did God do something incredible for me when he saved me, or did I do something incredible for him?* The right perspective matters when influencing others. If our faith is all about us, our choices, and our churches, then at best we will show Corinthians we have pride issues they hope never to have. But at worst we will put life in the kingdom on a shelf that they feel they cannot possibly reach. Our life with God should feature a testimony that includes, "If God can save *me*, he can save anybody."

Second, a kingdom agent must remember *Corinthians are normally pretty self-aware.* People are seldom blind to the depth of their own depravity. They know they should live better and make better choices. Their lives are one continual consequence of bad moral and relational decisions. But they are often so overwhelmed by their own messy lives that they become hopeless. Living out their own view of themselves with fatalistic attitudes, they believe there is no way out. And they know for sure a holy God would have little interest in the mess they created. Yet kingdom agents have personally experienced what a Corinthian does not think is possible. Their irreconcilable lives have been reconciled to God in Christ. They are living hope for the hopeless.

Third, a kingdom agent must remember *there are perfectly good reasons why Corinthians feel irreconcilable to God.* The most obvious is because without Christ they *are* irreconcilable. They live in constant guilt because they truly are guilty. The message from kingdom agents is one of hope but not false hope. I believe people who are on a spiritual journey to find Christ commonly need time and space. But I also know that "time and space" have consequences and are often overemphasized by cowardly believers. Truth will help fast-forward the spiritual journeys of the people we love. The gospel message is based on truth: Holy God has every reason to be angry with us. Christianity does not minimize, rationalize, or humanize our messy lives. Christianity offers a solution for the contradiction through reconciliation. Biblical Christianity faces and embraces the truth, and the truth is a person—Jesus Christ (John 14:6), who said, "You will know the truth, and the truth will set you free" (John 8:32). There is no citizenship in the kingdom without truth.

We are blessed so that we might be a blessing. We have kingdom responsibilities.

Praying a prayer of commitment and then biding one's lifetime with little more to keep ourselves grounded in Christian truth besides Sunday services and Christmas Eve is not the active, inspiring mission that animates a believer's day or invites others to join in the fun. It's not the logical response to Christ's transforming grace. It's not really even worth the effort of dealing with a nagging conscience if all we're going to do with our inner purity is just stand there and look at it, or perhaps quietly bemoan what it's keeping us from enjoying.

This all-too-common example of modern Christian witness is actually what's demotivating so many students from embracing their parents' faith today, leading them to choose other ways to frame their identity and fill in their time. Too many believers are ashamed, conflicted, and strangely distant from the God whom they claim means everything in the world to them. The true heart change that Christians wish to see in themselves (and in those they should be serving) is hindered because their authenticity is being counteracted by other interests, expectations, and fears.

It's empty.

It rings hollow.

On some levels nominal kingdom citizenship seems to be an easier, less invasive life. Yet ultimately it can't avoid meeting with circumstances that reveal just how unsteady and unsettling it really is. We are not left feeling ready for Christ's return or eager to see his rule take visible effect.

It is not our true kingdom self.

The people we're called to become in the "missing middle" are men, women, students, and teens who realize we've been entrusted by God with unique gifts and resources to be used in a daily, real-world struggle against the brokenness of the world. Filled with God's Spirit and attuned to human need, we rearrange our priorities to match his desires and plans for us in this time and space. Committed to being faithful to his singular claim on our lives, we orient our work, play, prayer, and attention so that we are constantly responding to his authority, eager to grow and get involved in his assigned tasks, seeking out those around us who are hurting and questioning, turning our "talents" into forms of everyday ministry that grow more natural and reflexive the more we invest ourselves in them.

"The kingdom of heaven is like" what happens when a master leaves his servants with tools to use in performing the work he has called them to do (Matt. 25:14 NKJV).

Sounds like, then, our call is to get about kingdom work. We were made alive to actually live for him.

5

Uncommonly Good

Bernie Madoff was uncommonly bad. He is not the first person in history to deserve that description, and neither will he be the last. Madoff, a Wall Street investment manager, was convicted of fraud as a result of stealing fifty billion dollars from investors. The Ponzi scheme (named after another uncommonly bad person) made Madoff a hated man and landed him in prison for 150 years. Evil gets a lot of publicity because when people steal billions of dollars or kill people (think Charles Manson), not only is it sensational but it is also uncommon.

We all struggle with doing the right thing and have done our share of wrong. But the majority of our bad is common bad. No policemen or cable news networks show up at our doorstep to get the real story. We may have an inappropriate sexual thought or may lose our temper occasionally with our spouse or children. We may leave early from work without permission or neglect other assigned responsibilities. The story we tell might be embellished or even changed in order to protect our agenda. But before I make you nervous, there is a point to be made here. Few of us are uncommonly bad. Our last names are not Madoff or Manson. We are not currently serving life sentences in prison.

So when it comes to self-assessment, we can so conveniently compare ourselves to the uncommonly bad. The comparison makes perfect sense. Let's keep Francis of Assisi and Billy Graham (or many others) out of this discussion. Let's focus on Bernie Madoff or Charles Manson. But the Bible put it all into perspective when Paul spoke to the Romans:

> What then? Are we any better? Not at all! For we have previously charged that both Jews and Gentiles are all under sin, as it is written: "There is no one righteous, not even one; there is no one who understands; there is no one who seeks God. All have turned away; all alike have become useless. There is no one who does good, not even one." (Rom. 3:9–12)

God's standard is complete conformity to his rule, which creates a dilemma for all of us. We do not have the luxury of comparing ourselves to the uncommonly bad.

But we do have another option. Let's just compare ourselves to the commonly good.

I may make you a little nervous again, but in my

experience most of the people I meet on a daily basis are good, at least by the standard definition used in my neighborhood. My personality or my passions may not match theirs. They may be uninteresting and even want to talk about things I couldn't care less about. But it is rare for me to meet people on a daily basis that I would not classify as good, sincere, hard-working, and who want the best for the world.

Their weird or awkward behavior may be incomprehensible to me, but they hold perfectly good reasons for the choices they make. And most of them are as perplexed by the Stetzer family as often as I am perplexed by their family. My neighbors are mostly good. The parents at my daughters' schools, as well as their kids, are mostly good. They do projects to feed and clothe the hungry. They volunteer hours to worthy causes in the community like soup kitchens or medical research. They often give donations to their churches, synagogues, mosques, and the local volunteer fire department. The portion of their paycheck that is withheld for the United Way is OK with them for the most part. They are what I call commonly good people.

But what if comparing ourselves to the uncommonly bad or the commonly good was not an option? Could there be a third option?

How about the *uncommonly good?*

The first time I heard the expression "uncommonly good" was in the '70s. You may connect the description to one of the most recognizable brands in America—Keebler cookies. Maybe I can jog your memory and give you the munchies at the same time: E. L. Fudge, Grasshoppers, Deluxe Grahams,

Rainbow Chocolate Chip. But remember why Keebler cookies were so uncommonly good? Because they were baked by elves who lived in a tree. The cookie story makes sense too. From uncommon origins come uncommon things . . . in this case, uncommonly good cookies.

As kingdom citizens we neither have the option of comparing ourselves to the high bar of uncommonly bad nor setting a low bar of the commonly good . . . much to our regrets. Kingdom citizens are pointed to an "uncommonly good" standard. But when you make the correct comparison to the absolute righteous standard of God and become incredibly overwhelmed by the impossibility of meeting that standard, you are close to a revolutionary spiritual breakthrough. We see the secret in John's Gospel with Jesus' words: "Remain in Me, and I in you. Just as a branch is unable to produce fruit by itself unless it remains on the vine, so neither can you unless you remain in Me" (John 15:4).

We cannot produce the fruit of an uncommonly good kingdom life by ourselves. Kingdom citizens have a King, and that King has given them new life. He literally birthed his subjects. And their absolute loyalty is to his reign and rule in their lives. He, in turn, gives the supernatural ability to make us uncommonly good because our lives come from him.

Something was uncommonly good about the first Christians after Pentecost. The unpopularity of Christians among religious people and governments becomes immediately apparent in the book of Acts. But there were other opinions beyond the religionists and governors. Brand-new Christians—kingdom citizens—were described as those who were "praising God and having favor with all the people. And every day the Lord added to them those who were being saved" (Acts 2:47).

I think it's incredible how the first believers praised God. Their lives were vitally connected to their heavenly Father, and they spoke freely about his greatness. No worship leader taught them how to praise God, yet they instinctively praised God. How awesome is it that God used them to convince others to be saved? Again, no soul winner's course was necessary. The natural (actually supernatural) overflow of their lives influenced others to be saved.

But a mysterious and uncommon description of these brand-new believers was sandwiched in between the praising and the saving: "having favor with all people." The word *favor* means "grace" in the original language and describes a pleasing, kind, and beautiful disposition. Something was uncommonly good and beautifully attractive about them. We are obsessed today with making our churches attractive to others. Yet the secret to the viral gospel influence of postresurrection kingdom citizens was not the meetings in their churches but their everyday lives. Were they better than the uncommonly bad people in Jerusalem? I guess so, but they weren't the only ones. Were they as good as the commonly good in Jerusalem? Yes again, but they were not alone. The Holy Spirit through the power of the resurrected Jesus placed something uncommon in them that was obvious to everybody. A quality never seen before that was uncommonly good.

Uncommon Behavior

We've already noticed a lot of things different about kingdom living from the run-of-the-mill average life—even from the standard-issue Christian life. For example, kingdom agents are as satisfied working in small, underreported places and contexts as they are in larger venues of service where they can leave at the end of the day with a T-shirt and a tax deduction.

Kingdom agents are willing to give up anything— *anything!*—that compromises their intensity for seeing God glorified and people brought face-to-face with the heart and soul of the gospel. They know where the real treasures of life are found. They know what true joy is.

Those transferred into the kingdom and living for the King don't sweat what they don't have. They are confident enough in how God provides for them and where he places them; they don't waste a lot of time wondering how their life would be better if they had more of the world's instruments. Kingdom agents aren't all talk; they're all God's. They don't make a big deal about what they do; they just do it.

They're just different.

They have to be.

You can't be subversive of the status quo if you *are* the status quo!

But if we're not careful, all this spiritual zeal and focus can mask something deeper that still needs addressing. The task of kingdom living is not merely comprised of differ-ent attitudes and priorities that result in different kinds of outreaches and ministries. As much as kingdom citizenship means championing a bold, new cause, it still means developing good, old-fashioned character. Yes, a kingdom heart must go to the bone.

To the words we say.

To the patience we show.

To the spouse we married.

To the habits we kick and the ones we hold on to.

The same kingdom mentality that alters our spiritual drive and initiative must also show up in our daily integrity.

This is the clear message that comes from Jesus' landmark Sermon on the Mount, where he employed his remarkable teaching methods to show us that countercultural thinking translates into countercultural living. Not only does he call us to proclaim the gospel and demonstrate its transforming power in action; he also makes clear that the gospel inherently produces a kingdom ethic for our lives—an ethic so different from that of the world, our adherence to it causes us to stand out as people with allegiance to another King. Simply by living like him and according to his principles, we secretly subvert the values and lifestyles that masquerade as normal in our culture.

We don't want to miss this. Jesus points us to kingdom action, and we are right to think in action-oriented ways. We are agents of that subversive kingdom, but we don't just subvert the order of the world by what we do; we subvert it by *who we are.*

We've talked much about what we do for the kingdom, but we must not miss who we are in the kingdom. Some people and groups want to talk a lot about changing society, and that's good. Others seem to talk about dealing with our own character problems—and that's good, too. Yet the Bible gives us a different picture when the apostle James writes, "Pure and undefiled religion before our God and Father is this: to look after orphans and widows in their distress and to keep oneself unstained by the world" (James 1:27).

A person who is changed becomes an agent of change. They continue to grow, learn, and serve because they themselves have been changed.

That's the intended influence of kingdom character.

Integrity Matters

Most, if not all, of the scenarios and situations Jesus covers in this extensive sermon are probably familiar to you. You've heard them taught. You've likely read them repeatedly. But all too often the nearness of a particular subject matter can gauze it from careful notice. So let's do ourselves a big favor at this point and alert our brain to its natural tendency. Let's settle back a little deeper into our chairs. Let's listen up. Let's be willing to do the hard work of connecting these teaching points of Jesus with actual, real-time events in our own lives, situations we may not have brought around here lately for any kind of scriptural scrutiny. Because if we do, we may find we're not only missing the mark; we're also missing some prime opportunities for letting God make a kingdom impression on people who know us and see us and aren't yet convinced he makes that much difference in a person's life.

You see, one of the great challenges today is that many people who have been made citizens of the kingdom look, well, like citizens of the world. Yet King Jesus is making a new people who live like *his* people. They are changed to be agents of the kingdom because they live differently—that's a mark of being a kingdom citizen. And it changes us. It changes the things in our lives. Jesus is unapologetic to connect who you are in Christ with how you live for Christ. Those things matter.

Things like our anger. You may or may not be the type of person who's easily upset or incited to high-volume reactions toward people who cross or challenge you. But none of us are immune from situations where the volatility of our tempers are put to the test and often found wanting. Whether from a line of questioning we don't particularly like at home, or an overeager driver at a four-way stop, or a policy change at the office that adds an extra layer of paperwork to an otherwise manageable process, we can feel the fire rising up our necks at any minute of the day. But a person under submission to the King knows that "everyone who is angry with his brother will be subject to judgment" (Matt. 5:22). And even with biblical allowances for being bluntly honest, direct, and holding others accountable, even with the reality of such things as justice and fairness, we cannot allow unchecked anger to simmer in our hearts if we expect to stay sharply subversive and spiritually on point. Controlling our anger proves we're different from the pack.

Things like our authenticity. Far too much of life is spent coordinating our public personas so they don't reveal certain private aspects of ourselves that we'd much rather stay under wraps and undealt with. Everyone has their skeletons, we surmise, and most people become fairly adept at dancing around them well enough so others don't notice. But Jesus says his people must be the kind who, for example, cannot worship devotedly on Sunday if they've been unkind or offensive toward someone through the week. "If you are offering your gift on the altar, and there you remember that your brother has something against you, leave your gift there in front of the altar. First go and be reconciled with your brother, and then come and offer your gift" (vv. 23–24). Being the same person both inside and out proves we're different.

Things like our purity. Not a man alive can honestly say he's never had an unguarded sexual thought or allowed a casual glance to morph into a cagey stare. And heaven knows, except for the awkward embarrassment of being caught looking, our society basically accepts this crude behavior as being part of what it means to be a guy. But in Jesus' way of seeing things, "everyone who looks at a woman to lust for her has already committed adultery with her in his heart" (v. 28). While we may never be able to extinguish entirely the temptation to let our eyes and imaginations wander, servants of the King allow him to transform their minds until they see their lust for how evil, demeaning, and ungodly it really is. Being a person who maintains a pure heart and honors his wedding vows—in both action and attitude—demonstrates that we're different.

Each of these are areas where we tend to rationalize our self-righteousness and excuse our behavior as being better than most. Sure, we try our hardest and do our best, but who can really keep from getting angry now and then, or being a bit hypocritical, or entertaining certain thoughts we wouldn't want others to know about? And yet Jesus, by bringing these matters to our attention and showing us a different way of handling them, declares that his kingdom is governed by a whole new value system. No, it's not the model that's on daily display in the homes, businesses, sports bars, and nightspots of our worldly culture. It's sadly not always the model that frequents our churches and youth retreats and Christian college groups either. But it's the model that's meant to define what kingdom life consistently looks like. It looks good on us.

And what looks good on us ultimately looks good on him.

Truth Be Told

But perhaps the one teaching of Jesus in this stretch of Matthew 5 that seems the most minor by comparison is the one that appears next—the one I'd like to spend the balance of this chapter discussing for it can show a fault line in our character—and point out how citizens of the kingdom live differently. For while it may appear more incidental than the others, even odd in its language and choice of examples, I believe it to be one of the key areas where we as Christ's kingdom agents can show forth the distinction of his rule in our lives.

God has a pattern of taking his people (in the Old and New Testaments) and giving them characteristics or a lifestyle that intentionally sets them apart. In a sense he puts them on display. One way we do that is by demonstrating how we stand out on even small things.

Like telling the truth.

Again, you have heard that it was said to our ancestors, "You must not break your oath, but you must keep your oaths to the Lord." But I tell you, don't take an oath at all: either by heaven, because it is God's throne; or by the earth, because it is His footstool; or by Jerusalem, because it is the city of the great King. Neither should you swear by your head, because you cannot make a single hair white or black. But let your word "yes" be "yes," and your "no" be "no." Anything more than this is from the evil one. (Matt. 5:33–37)

Our self-righteous temptation is to say, "Well, I've never done any of those things—sworn by heaven, sworn by the earth, sworn by Jerusalem—certainly not sworn by my own head!" But that's missing the larger point. What Jesus is addressing is our tendency to seek loopholes for our dishonesty, to exercise degrees of truthfulness, to wiggle out of awkward moments by making promises that sound sincere but really aren't.

The people of Jesus' day, not unlike our own, often said things they didn't mean and made promises they didn't intend to keep. But depending on how seriously they were committed to actually doing something they'd announced or made public to others, they usually felt inclined to raise the intensity of their promise to reflect the level of their certainty.

So if not even wild horses could keep them from fulfilling what they'd said, they might "swear to God"—make the most binding promise of all. If they were pretty sure about keeping their word but not wanting to feel totally hemmed in, they might swear by something a bit lesser—"by heaven," for example. If they meant to make good but wanted the freedom to easily and understandably change their minds if something unforeseeable should later arise, they might swear "by Jerusalem" or something a little closer to earth. And if they were more like fifty-fifty from the beginning anyway, they might only swear by an object as commonplace as their "own head." This promise didn't mean much, and everybody knew it.

In other words, just making a matter-of-fact statement wasn't the same as ensuring its accuracy. Telling the truth wasn't really expected; in fact, hedging one's bets was more the norm. And whether you're talking about first-century Palestine or modern-day wherever you are, these fast-and-loose treatments of truth are simply not kingdom principles. They're worldly values and tactics.

Several years ago, MSNBC reported an Associated Press/Ipsos poll that found more than half of respondents believed that lying was never justified. Sounds almost refreshing, doesn't it? Yet when answering another question in the same survey, 66 percent of them changed their tune a bit and said that lying *was* acceptable in certain situations, such as when trying to protect someone's feelings. In other words, people believe lying is wrong, but they lie anyway.

There's the world for you.

But is that not the world's perception of believers as well, based on the way too many of us operate?

Are we not often just as quick as everyone else to rationalize our dishonest statements (or dishonest silences) as being

105

some sort of higher road, a relative good, a result we can more easily live with than the high demands of total honesty? Of course we are. And it's easier that way. But King Jesus wants us to look different. Telling the truth all the time will do that to you. Trust me.

We often justify what we're doing by thinking, "Hey, no one will ever know," or we say, "The IRS already gets enough of my money, don't they?" Do we smile and say we'd love to get together for lunch sometime when we know good and well we'll never think about it again once this person walks away?

We rationalize degrees of truthfulness. We talk a lot, but we don't always engage our integrity. So doesn't that really mean we're hiding behind dishonest smokescreens meant to keep ourselves in full control rather than under our King's authority? Doesn't that mean we prefer being as comfortable as possible within our relationships and culture instead of being deliberately subversive and standing out?

When we speak the truth, we demonstrate the reality of this new life we've received, showing that Truth himself has set us free to be truth tellers (John 8:32)—that our King leads us by a different code of conduct. When we "speak the truth, each one to his neighbor" (Eph. 4:25), we shine as distinctive lights in a world where stopping short of honesty is always so much easier than being up-front. The reason we avoid swimming around within these varying degrees of truthfulness is because we've encountered the Truth and he has transformed us completely. Therefore, we don't need to gloss up our words with extra relish.

Our yes can be yes, and our no can be no.

Simple (and subversive) as that.

The youngest two of my three daughters are big on "pinky promises." When they link their little fingers together and agree on something between themselves or their friends, that's when you know it's getting serious, like—as they're apt to say—"If you break a pinky promise, I'll break your pinky, promise!" It's nothing to sneeze at. Bones will be broken. Which is why when I tell one of my girls that I'm taking her out fishing tomorrow, I don't "bite" when she tells me to make it a pinky promise. "Honey, if I say we're going to do it, then we're going to do it." We don't need to promise that our promise is good!

That's just the way kingdom people are supposed to live.

Again, it's not that Jesus was saying it's wrong to make a vow or an oath, like in a courtroom or at the wedding altar. Don't get lost in the legalistic mechanics here. Scripture actually offers plenty of examples where people communicated the depths of their convictions by means of an oath. Paul made an oath of sorts when he said, "I speak the truth in Christ—I am not lying; my conscience is testifying to me with the Holy Spirit" (Rom. 9:1). Even Jesus himself—when the high priest piously announced during his crucifixion trial, "By the living God I place You under oath: tell us if You are the Messiah, the Son of God!"—answered back, "You have said it" (Matt. 26:63–64). But the oath itself didn't have any bearing on whether or not they spoke the truth. Whatever they said was true, however they said it.

Yet we have to get this point: oaths exist in our culture because people routinely lie. But as agents of Christ's subversive kingdom, oaths are not needed to hold us more strongly accountable to our own statements. When people hear us talk, they should have no question that we're talking straight, that we're kingdom people, and that kingdom people are different. People notice people like that.

High Water Mark

Every day offers us opportunities for stretching the truth, withholding information, seeking a questionable advantage, or just outright lying. I clearly recall an event many years ago, for example, when life presented me with a situation that seemed tailor-made for beating the system.

I was sitting in my church office in Erie, Pennsylvania, where we had recently planted a young congregation, when rain started to fall in torrential amounts—seven or eight inches in the span of a few hours. Turning on the radio, I heard that many of the creeks and waterways around town were filling up and overflowing their banks, including the ones near the residential section where our low-lying apartment was located. Knowing how our little place was situated, I was sure it was probably taking on water, and our belongings were most likely at risk of being lost.

So I hopped in the car and sped home, only to find the police had already blocked off access to our neighborhood. But not being one to let a little thing like yellow tape or barricades stop me, I found a way around the roadblock and sloshed into our apartment to see the damage for myself, to see if I could salvage anything.

Fortunately, I discovered that the floodwaters were still contained to the basement area. (Technically, I found out later that it was drain backup from the flood.) The waters hadn't yet reached the main floor and didn't look like they would. I was fortunate also because as recently as a few weeks earlier my insurance agent had convinced me to buy some extra coverage, meaning that in the event of a situation like this, we would still be eligible for replacement benefits. Good timing, huh!

But time was not on my side at the moment. The water was rising downstairs and our stuff was submerging, with the exception of a few items on a higher shelf. Most of it, granted, wasn't worth much—like the majority of things that get hauled down to the basement. We didn't really need it; we just hadn't known where else to put it. But one of the more valuable pieces of equipment I spotted was a high-quality printer that was resting on that top shelf, still above the water line by about six inches!

I had bought that printer when we first started the church, spending hundreds of dollars we couldn't afford so we could have the capability of generating fancy flyers, newsletters, and posters. It was a lifesaver and a real help to our communication needs. But the printer had quit working not too many months before, and I had taken it down to the basement until I could scrounge up enough time and money to get it repaired.

And now . . . there it sat. Water lapping below, a few tantalizing inches from its base. If it were to fall in or be overtaken by the flood level, insurance would cover the full cost of replacing it. Jesus would get a brand-new one—courtesy of my insurance company. All that stuff we hadn't been able to do or create since the printer went down could be back up and running in no time. *Yes, Lord!*

So get the picture: here was the pastor, looking across the room at a piece of church property in his waterlogged basement, thinking, "You know what? I can't lie, but technically it wouldn't really be lying if the printer got wet."

You see, I had no intention of actually wading over and pushing it into the water. I'm not that kind of a guy! But anything could happen, couldn't it? The shelf could fall, water could slosh up on it as I walked toward it, mildew could cause corrosion to its inner workings before I had a chance to remove it from the premises. No one could say I was to blame if it got damaged like that. If I started moving around and the water picked up a little more velocity, it would be covered. Honestly.

Well, maybe not *honestly*.

Isn't that what Jesus was really talking about? People were setting up scenarios where they weren't required to keep their word or tell the truth. They were swearing by things they had no control over—the heavens, the earth, the city where the temple stood. They were able to blame everyone and everything if they went back on a promise or skewed things a different way than they'd led others to believe they would. But we *do* have control over whether or not we'll live with truthful integrity, even when a situation arises where a small lie could save us a big headache. We *do* have control over how we follow through on the commitments we make. We *do* have control over the words we say (and don't say) and the manner in which we carry them out.

We have a different King.

He rules a different kingdom.

We represent his different way.

We've all been inspired by soldiers who possess an uncommon code of honor, who fulfill their orders and stay true to their duties at great cost to themselves, against incredible odds. They cling to their integrity because they are serving their superiors, defending their country, protecting something bigger than themselves.

And it's no different with spiritual citizens of God's subversive kingdom. Thanks to who we are and whom we serve, we live by a different ethic. We're honest in a way the world finds just crazy. We're dependable. We're known as people who keep our word. We don't settle for having a certain "truthiness" in the things we say, like too many politicians and other leaders communicate through their speech and demeanor. We're just truthful. We say what we mean. We stay under authority. Our yes is yes, and our no is no. And in a world like ours, that is subversive indeed.

Kingdom living is not just what we do; it's also who we are.

The King's Standard

The whole Gospel of Matthew is about Jesus as King. In the first chapter we see his human ancestry traced through the kingly line of David. In Matthew 2 we see Herod feeling threatened by the mysterious prospect of a new king on the rise, and we see the magi bringing royal gifts to honor his arrival. Then by Matthew 5, when we hear him laying out the descriptive plan for how his kingdom is supposed to be entered and what his subjects are supposed to look like, we recognize that we are not up to the challenge he advances. We've all failed him in so many ways. We can't keep his requirements to the level he demands. We are incapable of living with the integrity he has called us to embody.

It's frustrating.

It's discouraging.

But this kingdom integrity challenge is not about a mere change of behavior or the completion of a self-improvement course. Jesus' teaching in the Sermon on the Mount does not insist that we do these things on our own but that we recognize our need for his sanctifying empowerment. The only way we can truly represent our King and his kingdom is not by gutting out our obedience but by letting his righteousness pour through our poor attempts at following him. It is less about making resolutions and more about surrendering to his authority. If his resurrection power does not pound in our hearts, we cannot possibly live in such a way that honors him and makes known his glory.

So, yes, this disturbingly tall standard is here. It's always here and it's not going away. The standard is much higher and much different than the standard of this world. In fact, the demands of his kingdom say that we must be "perfect," as our heavenly Father is perfect (Matt. 5:48)—everyone from fiery redheads to regular old Freds—growing into a "mature man with a stature measured by Christ's fullness" (Eph. 4:13).

Wherever you fail to see his integrity taking hold in your life, make this a matter of deep repentance and renewal. Recognize what happens in the lives of those around you when you fail to be humble, authentic, and pure; when those already deceived by lies do not see truth lived out even in the people of God. Enter the throne room of your King in prayer tonight, laying down your independent streak and picking up what he alone can do to change your values and desires.

Is your heart in his hands? Then his integrity can grow from your fingertips. It's not something we do on our own— trying harder to be a good person. Yet with the kingdom transfer we've had, we received a new life, and this new life can be lived through the work of Christ on the cross and the power of the spirit. Through him you can be uncommonly good . . . and point a confused world toward the risen King who will one day make all things perfect.

6

Rules of Engagement

Living in between the "already, but not yet" calls for citizens of God's kingdom to respond differently to the people and circumstances we encounter around us. In the last chapter we looked at how his standards affect our personal integrity, the way we orient our hearts so we respond to life's temptations with patience, truth, and purity. In this chapter we'll turn to the back half of Matthew 5 to see how these same, subversive values transform not only our inner attitudes but also our treatment of others.

Another important step in constructing our kingdom selves is relationships. God has made relationships his chosen delivery system for the gospel of hope. God uses Bibles and tracts to communicate his message in certain places, but the impact of God's information in black and white is influenced by the people who bear the information. Relationally dysfunctional kingdom citizens are terrible advertisements for life with God being a better way.

Moving on to something easier or more sensational would probably be your preference at this point. The woman at the well in John 4 could relate. When Jesus addressed the issue of her five previous husbands and current live-in domestic partner, she turned quickly to something deeper and more fun to talk about. Beginning with an overstatement of comedic proportions, she said, "I see that You are a prophet. Our fathers worshiped on this mountain, yet you Jews say that the place to worship is in Jerusalem" (John 4:19–20). Ed's translation: "Enough about me and my life. Let's talk about something more comfortable like a deep theological issue."

Jesus dug in deep to the relational ethic of the kingdom. He pointed his disciples to what kingdom living looks like. And if he took the time to tell us, we would do well to take the time to tell one another, reminding ourselves that the kingdom of God shapes how we relate to others around us.

And this step is truly, radically subversive because people are accustomed to a certain way of relating to others, one that usually requires great effort and watchfulness on their part if they wish to maintain their advantage. They expect others to be resistant and hard to work with. They know to be ready for unreasonable opposition to their points and preferences. They're braced for mechanics and repairmen who are apt to run up a bill or do shoddy work. Even if others are kind to their face, they feel sure the person is probably thinking something else underneath, if not freely raking them over the coals the next time an opportunity arises.

That's how the game works.

But that's because they primarily deal all day with people who operate from worldly principles and selfish motivations. They're trained to live, work, and maintain relationships within a culture that overvalues personal rights and privacy, undervalues the contributions of others, and doesn't typically extend a lot of unexpected favors unless it benefits the giver somehow. Every day is another exercise in survival, and they don't expect others to bend over backwards to help them meet their objectives. Because if it means someone else going out of their way to do it, they'll probably just end up having to take care of it themselves.

That's life the way most people know it.

Now . . . enter those who live by the values of a subversive kingdom.

Our King has both told us and shown us how a truly transformed individual can step into the public arena each morning on a mission to overturn the status quo and shake up the way people think. When a believer's response to difficulty, challenge, insult, and unfairness differs sharply from what the world expects and is used to seeing—even in other Christians—that person is setting off kingdom sparks that attract attention and raise all kinds of interesting questions. Christ-inspired goodness and sacrifice, when done with a smile and a genuine desire to bless and spread blessing, almost always send a message that can't be preached in a Sunday sermon. Acting in ways that may seem foolish, unnecessary, even bizarre to the unsuspecting recipients of our selfless love can open doors for us to explain what causes us to behave like this—like our King and his kingdom.

It takes us beyond mere belief and into mighty, subversive action.

Beyond Belief

Again, Jesus prefaced his teaching in the Sermon on the Mount with common misunderstandings from Old Testament law and culture, revealing that people have always tended to gravitate toward baseline obedience and minimum requirements. When God said, for example, in Exodus, Leviticus, and Deuteronomy that the victim's code for responding to personal injury was "an eye for an eye and a tooth for a tooth," as Jesus quoted (Matt. 5:38), he was never endorsing vengeful, vigilante justice. In reality, he was actually placing *limits* on people's tendency to inflict damage on another's person or property that went far beyond the original offense. He was restricting the reach of their retribution. Without such a limit, someone who had suffered any amount of loss might say or think in anger, "I'll kill you for this"—a retaliatory approach to wrongdoing that was commonplace in the ancient Middle East. God's word to his Old Testament people, however, was meant to communicate that punishment must fit the crime. Justice was a person's right, yes, but nothing further. No "overkill."

Jesus, however, introduced an advanced level of response that went beyond measured retribution, even *rightful* retribution. One of the best ways, he said, to make an impact for his kingdom—a way to engage with others in a real-world manner that speaks people's language and advances God's mighty revolution on earth—is by responding to mistreatment in a strong, controlled, countercultural fashion. Paul captured it like this:

> Friends, do not avenge yourselves; instead, leave room for His wrath. For it is written: "Vengeance belongs to Me; I will repay," says the Lord. But "if your enemy is hungry, feed him. If he is thirsty, give him something to drink. For in so doing you will be heaping fiery coals on his head." Do not be conquered by evil, but conquer evil with good. (Rom. 12:19–21)

It's just a new way to respond. The kingdom way. New rules of engagement.

And watch out: *they work.*

Remember—from the parable of the weeds, if not from the realities of this past *week*—that life in the kingdom of God means we currently coexist with people who have the ability to hurt us, ignore us, malign us, and repeat rude things about us. They are often given to questioning our motives, falsely judging our actions, challenging our convictions, and misunderstanding what we say. They can sometimes disagree with us just because they don't like us. They can enjoy seeing us in uncomfortable situations, thinking we're getting what we deserve. They can eat us for lunch. They can kick us when we're down.

But nothing and no one can force us off our kingdom-imposed mandate. And because the Lord Jesus is involved in stirring these Christlike actions into life in us—beyond our own capabilities—we can be confident he will accomplish his purposes through our humble responses toward others.

Let's look at several of these. You *know* them well, but do they *describe* you well?

1. Turn the other cheek. "I tell you, don't resist an evildoer. On the contrary, if anyone slaps you on your right cheek, turn the other to him also" (Matt. 5:39). If this sounds completely unreasonable to you, it's possible that part of your contention is based on a misinterpretation of the verse. Most people tend to believe this familiar colloquialism means we should never defend ourselves or our family or resist evil in any form. If someone does something ugly, underhanded, or upsetting to us, we're just supposed to take it, whatever it is.

But don't forget that the same person who said this is the one who drove conniving, profiteering merchants from the temple grounds. With a whip. He's the same one whose Word shrewdly teaches us that "a righteous person who yields to the wicked is like a muddied spring or a polluted well" (Prov. 25:26).

We're not helpless to take up for ourselves, not even by biblical command.

In fact, the people who originally heard Jesus speak these words would have known immediately he wasn't suggesting they expose themselves or their loved ones to physical harm from a home intruder. In their culture striking someone on the right cheek was just a visible way of expressing a dismissive, insulting attitude toward the other person. In some modern societies showing the bottom of one's foot is a similar affront. In today's Western context it might be akin to rolling one's eyes at somebody, speaking in a condescending tone, acting like we're too busy to listen, or any comparable action that's meant to communicate obvious superiority toward the other. These are the "slaps" of Jesus' day, intended more for internal insult than external impact.

Digs. Putdowns. "Sure, fine, whatever."

Kingdom citizens need to realize that when we're on the receiving end of these kind of ugly remarks or unfounded rumors, the only thing that really suffers is our personal pride. And you know what? We can stand to live without that—more than we can afford to bring disrepute on the name of Christ by returning blow for blow. When we do, we pass up the chance to handle such a situation with noticeable kingdom poise and perspective.

Such encounters are opportunities for us to stop and ask ourselves an important question: *How do I avoid escalating this conflict and diffuse it instead?* That's not how the world generally reacts, but that's how a subversive thinks.

We carry around an agenda designed to get the kingdom of God both brought up in conversation and brought down to earth. And letting an insult bounce off without leaving a visible mark is one secret way to do that. It demonstrates that we consider our identity secure in God and in his rule rather than in whatever value other people attribute to us. To put it in biblical terminology, "In God I trust. . . . What can man do to me?" (Ps. 56:4). "The one who believes in Him will never be put to shame" (1 Pet. 2:6).

I wish this was how I always lived, but I must confess . . . it isn't. Not too long ago, in fact, one of our neighbors decided to make an issue about something that seemed small and oversensitive to me, and I reacted in a less-than-kingdom manner. I can appreciate the fact that some people take great pride in their manicured lawns, and I understand that property lines are legal boundaries duly enforceable by their owners. But look, I like to get out in the yard with my girls and have a big time. And while I do tell the kids, of course, to be careful not to leave messes in other people's yards, I'm not too concerned when they range out of bounds a little to chase the dog or retrieve a ball or whatever. One of my neighbors, however, *was* concerned about it. And one day, he (very kindly, I'll admit) asked if I'd be more careful about keeping my children off his grass.

Well, I probably shouldn't have, but I took that as an insult.

No, I didn't say anything I would regret. I didn't tell him my kids were too good to play in his yard anyway (though that's true), that he ought to be thankful he has such cute, smart, articulate girls around to breathe some real life into his mundane existence. But I did *think* it. And I'm sure at least some of it showed on my face. When I got back in the house and started talking to my wife about it, the more irritated I became. This guy had really gotten on my nerves, and I started to think up retaliation plans.

Our hearts naturally want to escalate offenses, even when the other person is somewhat or perhaps even totally justified in bringing an offense to our attention. If we take it wrong, our gut reaction is to return "evil for evil" and have fun while we do.

And yet if a desire to be nice or avoid conflict isn't enough to make us step back and shrug it off, let the following motivation be what presses us into Christian compliance: *we want the kingdom made visible in our lives.* We want to model the values of the Prince of peace, right out there where even a perfect pagan can see it. Or a loudmouthed coworker. Or even a fellow church committee member. By diffusing anger from the situation and infusing peace instead, we quietly undermine the devil's hold on people who are accustomed to dealing in retribution. Turning the other cheek can turn a slap into a subversive opportunity.

2. Give what's asked for . . . and more. "As for the one who wants to sue you and take away your shirt, let him have your coat as well" (Matt. 5:40). Again, a little context is called for, since our dress codes are obviously a lot different from those of Jesus' time. Wearing a "shirt" and "coat" (or a "tunic" and "cloak," to cite another translation) was just the customary layering of clothes in that culture. It was like having a topcoat over another coat. And if someone (for whatever reason) felt obliged to take your overcoat in repayment for a debt or some perceived offense, Jesus said the most extraordinary thing to do—rather than telling him "no way"—would be to see if going beyond his request would settle the matter once and for all.

Hear me, Jesus is still not suggesting that we leave our doors unlocked and our keys in the ignition, letting people walk all over us without a whimper. He's saying that if by taking the proactive initiative of one extra step—giving even a bit more than what was asked for—we can shrink an escalating standoff down to handshake size or even eliminate the disharmony altogether, we're striking real blows for the kingdom. We're doing more than just being creative and conciliatory; we're letting Christ make a big, bold statement through us.

The world may say, "Stand up for your rights; don't let them get the best of you." But the kingdom agent says, "I've got more to gain by giving this up than by holding it back."

The most reflexive response to finding yourself in disagreement with someone is to make your point and then stand on it. Don't budge off of it. See who blinks first, and be sure it's not you. But most disagreements are birthed by misunderstandings. And therefore often—with everyone dug into their positions like that—no amount of meet-in-the-middle agreement can ever be enough to end the altercation to everyone's satisfaction. Usually the only way to achieve peace and resolution is for one side to be magnanimous enough to go overboard. To pay back double. Not only to fix the presenting problem but offer to fix another one as well. To pop a gaping hole in the proceedings with a nice note, a free dinner, or a gift card to their favorite store.

To double the diffusion.

To make a person wonder who your King is.

A couple of years ago, a new church in Concord, North Carolina, experienced the great fear of every Christian fellowship who's meeting in portable, set-up facilities: *someone stole their trailer.* This is a big deal if you are a portable church.

I'm planting such a church right now, so I can definitely relate. We pull our own trailer up to the theater every Sunday where we meet. Without it, we'd have no nursery, no lyrics, no speakers, and a lot of other necessary stuff.

Yet in the blink of an overnight burglary, nearly everything they owned—their Bibles, their nursery stuff, their Communion trays, their speakers, their hospitality items, their weekly needs—all of it was gone. Big problem. Expensive to replace and really hard for them to do without. But rather than hunting down the perpetrator and pressing charges, the leaders of Kinetic Church decided they'd do something else: try reaching out to the alleged thief . . . and forgive him.

They were first able to receive free, donated space on five billboards around town, speaking directly to the thief and telling him their intentions. The resulting buzz even got some local TV coverage and a chance to tell their story to a broader audience. The pastor, Dave Milam, then recorded a YouTube video (http://www.youtube.com/watch?v=eL-LU0pxBhU), telling the man where he could find a disposable cell phone with which to call them, hoping to set up a meeting time and place so that just these two—the thief and the pastor—could sit down privately somewhere, share a meal, and talk about what Christ's love and mercy is all about with no judgment or consequences whatsoever.

No surprise, I guess, there's not a storybook ending to this cool little story. No meeting. No confession. No grand finale. (Not yet anyway.) But tell me if generating online feedback and comments like these don't leave their own little kingdom story to tell.

- "What a beautiful demonstration of God's forgiveness! So inspiring!"
- "I'm not religious, but even I want to go to that church."
- "I was amazed when I found this video on YouTube because when I took the picture of this [billboard] today I was going to use it as an example of the hatred and animosity of Christianity. Boy, did I feel judgmental when I saw this. I hope you get your stuff back, man. Your message is beautiful, and I respect your dignity during a difficult time."
- "Can you imagine how many souls could be saved if we all were THAT forgiving and loving and accepting of people who hurt us?! Amazing."
- "Thank you for so publicly demonstrating what God's unconditional love and forgiveness is like to a world who desperately needs it daily."

That's some serious gospel subversion going on. And while a lot of people miss the point of it, make light of it, or try to see something sneaky or manipulative in it, the fact remains that God's unrivaled rule and reign will find time in the spotlight when his people take the deliberate initiative to do more than what's expected of them.

One of the greatest things I've learned in life is this: *people are more important than the point.* Instead of working so hard to defend our positions and enforce our demands, we can till up a lot more kingdom soil by treating other people as more valuable than our own appeals for fairness and justice. Yes, we may see things differently than they do; and, yes, we may even be right. But our King has set the standard high enough that when people see the church and its people living the way he's instructed us, they will see what his kingdom is really all about.

3. *Walk a little farther.* "If anyone forces you to go one mile, go with him two" (Matt. 5:41). Israel in the first century was occupied by Roman forces, and Roman law held sway across the empire—like this one, for example: if a soldier was moving things from one place to another, he could instruct a Jewish male to carry his pack a full mile. "Just do it." And as you can imagine, this ordinance irritated the daylights out of most Israelite men who saw it as nothing other than a symbol of oppression at the hands of their occupiers.

Jesus had an alternative for them, however. Instead of inwardly detesting their sworn enemy while begrudgingly, legalistically hauling his gear an exact linear mile, they could choose instead to graciously carry his pack *two* miles. They'd get to spend more time talking with him and relating to him that way, while also giving him the chance to see that the King of their kingdom can change people's want-to, not just their gotta-do.

Like the "tunic and cloak" command before, do more than what's required.

It's revolutionary. It might seem crazy. It certainly makes you stand out—which is, I think, part of the point.

Wouldn't you agree that in the gospel we see God doing way more than what's required of him? The biblical writers speak of his grace as being abundant and extravagant

(Eph. 2:4), something he's "lavished on us with all wisdom and understanding" (1:8). In trying to capture the grand scope of his grace and the excessiveness of what he has done for us in Christ Jesus, I've used a short definition of the gospel:

> The gospel is the good news that God, who is more holy than we can imagine, looked with compassion upon people who are more sinful than we would possibly admit, and sent Jesus into history to establish his kingdom and reconcile people and the world to himself. Jesus, whose love is more extravagant than we can measure, came to sacrificially die for us so that by his death and resurrection, we might gain through his grace what the Bible defines as new and eternal life.

If our life is meant to be a daily response to a redemptive God who's gone to these kinds of extremes to establish relationship with us, then on what grounds do we declare ourselves exempt from being just like him? Haven't his indescribably generous actions communicated volumes to us about his character and purpose? Then what kind of chapters and paragraphs, at least, might our semiexorbitant acts of grace toward others tell them about this King who desires to rule in their hearts as well, just as he rules in ours?

Let's just be willing to walk a little farther with people.

When we hold our rights and privileges too tightly and refuse to let anyone take advantage of us, when we resist opening ourselves up to being hurt or disappointed—under any circumstances—we do not live as one who's on the receiving end of God's grace. But when we allow the needs of others to take precedence over ours, breaking the rules of a society that automatically defaults to looking out for number one, we subvert the kingdom of the world and show his prisoners what it's like to live in freedom and unexplainable joy.

4. *Show generosity.* "Give to the one who asks you, and don't turn away from the one who wants to borrow from you" (Matt. 5:42). Pretty bold words for people who live in a world that basically says, "Get what you can, and can what you get." The choice to live a cheerful, generous lifestyle, looking for ways to do more and want less, is a clear, defining mark of the subversive kingdom agent.

But while not wanting to prevent you from feeling God's conviction on giving him full control of your money and not wanting to slow down any ideas that come to mind when considering what he might do with a more generous *you*, it's probably wise at this point to balance this teaching with a fair word of caution.

Observe the tens and even hundreds of thousands of dollars that can be emotionally stirred up by the damage of a natural disaster in a coastal state or a small island nation. Think back to how many times the efforts and sacrifices of many people—sincere and dedicated as they may be—have resulted in money that never actually reaches its destination, is calved off through governmental corruption, or ends up being spent on supplies that aren't needed and go to waste. This is not necessarily a reason to cynically sit on your resources and avoid acting, especially when God is leading you to give and serve for a dire situation like that. But it does point out the fact that sometimes in our zeal to help and bring comfort, we can be unwise with what God has given us to share. I'm just saying we have to be careful. We need to be discerning.

Making a dent in the personal poverty of a certain region of the world, the nation, or a nearby neighborhood is a worthy goal. That's good. Wanting to minister to the physical needs of hurting people is a noble thing for God's people to do. But when you, your church, or a group of your Christian friends feel drawn to a particular cause, or when confronted with a face-to-face appeal on the street to meet an immediate need, stop and ask yourself: *What's really the best way to help them? And what should I expect from the people I'm assisting?*

Any work of ours that's undertaken without being thoroughly infused with kingdom principles and goals can often do more harm than good. Again, this is not an excuse for hanging back; it's just a little warning to be sure you're being the most faithful and effective with your time and money. The world system, engaged and entrenched in rebellion, doesn't take lightly our assaults on the dying, decaying kingdom or its suffering subjects, and we shouldn't enter into them lightly either.

Remember, the chief goal of our giving is kingdom work and gospel insurgency. Make sure when God taps your heart with an opportunity for being unusually generous, you do it according to his plans and purposes, not just because it's popular or comes with a cool benefit concert.

I don't think we can read the Gospels and not get that Jesus cares for the poor. So when I engage in generous giving to the poor, I am just doing what King Jesus modeled and called me to do. Each month when we send money (beyond our church giving) to our "adopted" Compassion child,[1] or we give more to finance a microbusiness through Kiva,[2] or we give though our denomination's "hunger fund,"[3] that's causing me to live more fully as a kingdom citizen.

Oh, and one more thing on this subject: know that sharing the generous, open lifestyle of the kingdom with others is as much about the state of your heart as the size of your wallet. Even as Christians, we can tend to view our charitable acts and giving as if we're the "haves" helping the "have-nots"—the financially stable stooping down to the less well off. In reality, poverty is a universal sign of sin's effects on our whole society, including ourselves. Each of us has been affected by the fall, and every one of us stands in desperate need before the Father. So when we actively step out to serve others, let's remember we are needy people helping other needy people. We are like the proverbial beggar telling another beggar where to find bread. We may not have the *same* needs, but we all have *many* needs. And kingdom people must always be quick to realize—deep down and more genuinely each day—that our ability to reach out is fueled and funded only by the generous hand of King Jesus reaching out to us.

So give, yes. Obey, yes. Make generosity an ongoing lifestyle and response. *Yes!* But unlike the often self-centered, here-and-there motivations of a sometimes giving world, the reason why we give is because we're cooperating with Christ's kingdom purposes on earth. He cares for the poor, so we care for the poor. That's a big difference that makes an eternal difference.

Love Your Enemies

We're familiar enough with Jesus' sermon to know he saved the best for last in Matthew 5. Well, maybe not the best but certainly the hardest.

"You have heard that it was said, 'Love your neighbor' and hate your enemy. But I tell you, love your enemies and pray for those who persecute you" (vv. 43–44). The part about "loving your neighbor" was an Old Testament imperative, but "hating your enemy" appears to have been tacked on later as somebody's implied logic. *If God said to love your neighbor, then surely it follows . . .*

Hmm. Not so fast.

Jesus says "love" goes all the way around.

But what do we really know about love? We use the same word to describe all kinds of emotional feelings. We love our spouse; we love our dog; we love good ice cream. *Love* means a lot of different things to us. So it's no wonder that we inch up to Jesus' statement thinking this "love" he says we're supposed to have for our enemies can't really be the same kind of love we have for a best friend.

No, that's *exactly* what he's saying.

If we expect to be well-trained, high-performing agents of God's kingdom—those who are known as "sons" of their "Father in heaven" (v. 45)—we must ask him to give us his love for everyone, enemies included. The same God who "causes His sun to rise on the evil and the good" and "sends rain on the righteous and the unrighteous" commands us to live for the welfare of all people, even the ones we don't like, even the ones who don't like us.

Like you, perhaps, I've experienced the need to love an enemy. To be fair, this enemy was not like an enemy we see around the world, where Christians are persecuted and killed for their faith. My enemy was a bit like a nemesis—a guy I worked for and grew to despise. And the feeling was mutual. It had started with a minor insult but had escalated into something much more volatile. (I should have listened to my own "turn the other cheek" teaching, huh!) Twice we had literally gotten up into each other's face, mad as hornets, nearly coming to blows. To say it had gotten serious was an understatement. People knew about it across the country. And to make matters worse, we were both employed in training pastors at a Christian seminary. I was a professor; he was the dean. We weren't setting a good example for anyone, much less representing our King very well.

Finally, after three years of putting up with this mess, I decided I'd been through enough. I took a new job in Atlanta, packed up my family, and hoped to leave Thom Rainer behind for good. Everything seemed to be working out great. New life—no Thom.

Yet God was convicting me. And I found out later, he was working on Thom, too.

One day I came across an article Thom had written that was exceptionally well done. Really good stuff. And try as I might to squelch what felt like God's persuasive nudging in my spirit, I decided I should sit down and write my nemesis an e-mail—tell him what I thought of this editorial piece and also tell him what I'd been thinking lately in regard to our simmering conflict. "Thom," I began, still not sure I wanted to do this, "I know we didn't get along very well at the seminary, but I just wanted to let you know I thought your article was great. You're a key voice right now in what God is doing."

Short. Sweet.

Click. Send.

Within a matter of minutes, Thom wrote back to say something like, "Thanks, Ed. We did have some rough times, I know, but I appreciate your comments." And from the ashes of a scorched working relationship, God began to reconcile what we two tough guys had managed to destroy. We changed our rules of engagement, and the Lord changed *us* in the process. Fighters became brothers. Enemies became friends.

And now, as they say, the rest is history; we are both in Nashville, and he is my boss.

Again.

A pretty incredible thing happens inside when you start praying for another person. Your heart changes toward him. The Scripture really starts convicting and challenging you. Through the infilling power of God, you begin to want something that doesn't come naturally. You want what's best for this person, to wish him well, to work for his good. To love him.

Love is never birthed out of some benign affirmation, like, "I know we're supposed to love everybody." In a world order based on manipulative, opponent-crushing self-interest, love doesn't make much difference until it's motivated by kingdom truth, until we intentionally, proactively sail past all our reasons for withholding it and choose instead to extend God's grace to others. Even our enemies.

Now that's subversive.

So turn the other cheek. Give a little extra. Go the second mile. Don't hold back. Because when kingdom agents start deliberately letting God do these kinds of remarkable things through them—hard as it can be to do them—they've found some of the best ways to shake up their surroundings. They've found their kingdom self.

7

Idol Elimination

I've seen lots of idols in my time. From statues in India, and masks in Africa, to ancestral markings in South America, idols exist in all shapes and sizes. All forms of idols fill gaps. Man was designed to worship and *will* worship something. And as strange as these items may appear, it's not hard to notice their power. They capture the identities of those who are so connected to these attachments from their culture and history.

Yet strangely enough, *my* idols are not strange to *me*.

They call to me. Personally. They appeal to me from my past. They make their persuasive case for why I need them so badly and how much they can do for me. They try to convince me that we can all get along here in one place together, that I can share space with both them and my Christian devotion at the same time, and that God will understand.

So my idols are much more personal than a piece of stone or a block of wood. Anything from my past or present that shapes my identity or fills my thoughts with something other than God, especially on a regular, ongoing, irresistible basis, is an idol. Idolatry does not count the cost of worshipping anything but God. And although few of us could ever imagine worshipping a picture of ourselves, the reality is—we are either worshipping God or some form of ourselves. When we are driven by physical and emotional appetites rather than being led by the Spirit of God, we are worshipping the idol of ourselves. Paul spoke as a prophet on fire to the Colossian Christians: "Therefore, put to death what belongs to your worldly nature: sexual immorality, impurity, lust, evil desire, and greed, which is idolatry" (Col. 3:5).

Both a king and his kingdom exist in every person's life, creating within us an impulse or desire for something more than we have right now. Even many God-given desires can turn into idols when we become too urgent to satisfy those desires. But every idol is a competitor. Our kingdom calling will always be mutually exclusive with the conniving appeals of other gods. We must never forget that we are in "rebellion against the rebellion" of the world's system, that we are commissioned by God to live with different loyalties from those of the world—and that, in fact, part of our motivation for choosing this singular existence is for the *sake* of those who are caught in the enemy's trap.

We're just subversive that way, aren't we?

Because if we allow idols to occupy living quarters in our hearts—especially on a consistent, unquestioned basis—we will never be able to develop the integrity and discernment necessary to challenge the oppressive values of the broader culture. We'll be too distracted and self-absorbed to notice the many examples of pain, doubt, confusion, and injustice happening in people's lives right around us. We simply cannot serve successfully as agents for the kingdom of light while simultaneously harboring pockets of darkness in the shadows and corners of our hearts. Just can't. Doesn't work like that.

Idols. Divided loyalties. Split personalities.

These are things we cannot tolerate if we hope to remain subversive.

Inside the Idol Factory

Idols are the gods of our rebellious world. Just as the church exists on earth as an outpost of the kingdom of light (which we'll discuss far and wide in the final section of the book), idols are visible outposts of the kingdom of darkness. Idols are localized expressions of the world's values that seek to replace King Jesus with their own rule.

Paul confronted the issue during a stopover in Athens: "While Paul was waiting for them in Athens, his spirit was troubled within him when he saw that the city was full of idols. So he reasoned in the synagogue with the Jews and with those who worshiped God and in the marketplace every day with those who happened to be there" (Acts 17:16–17).

Paul did not ignore the obvious, but I am impressed with the fact that "his spirit was troubled within him." May we never grow comfortable with idolatry in and around us that not only ruins lives but, if not resolved, will send people to hell for eternity. We learn so much about Paul as a kingdom citizen by his response in Athens. Paul was not driven by the duties, oughts, and shoulds of religious life. Those days were history for him. Paul was driven by *lostness*. He made some incredible from-the-heart statements about his obsession with lost people, talking about the "intense sorrow" and "continual anguish" he felt in his heart for them. "I could wish to be cursed and cut off from the Messiah for the benefit of my own flesh and blood" (Rom. 9:2–3). Are you amazed at his heart for the lost? He volunteered, if possible, to be "cut off from the Messiah" if he thought his brothers would accept Christ. Willing to go to hell so they would not? Really?

Wayne Cordeiro, pastor of New Hope Christian Fellowship in Honolulu, expressed his love for lost people and his involvement in their rescue. In explaining the greatness of spending eternity in heaven with Jesus, he presented a sobering thought:

> But of all the trillions of surprises, there's one thing we will never see again for all of eternity. We will never see another non-Christian. Right now, in this life, we have the only opportunity to usher people to the Forgiver. Our lifetime contains the only possibility for us to play an active part in God's plan of salvation for others.[1]

Paul knew that embracing Jesus as Lord in one arm with an armful of idols in the other was a contradiction. So he held nothing back for such an important task. The souls of men were at stake. Heaven could not wait for people to get their minds or lives straight before they came to Jesus. Paul openly challenged their idolatry: "What agreement does God's sanctuary have with idols? For we are the sanctuary of the living God, as God said: 'I will dwell among them and walk among them, and I will be their God, and they will be My people'" (2 Cor. 6:16).

The space is only so wide for others' relationship with Jesus to begin and develop. The time for us to influence their salvation is not infinite. So kingdom agents cannot afford the luxury of being distracted by their own idols, nor can they be intimidated by the idols that are keeping others from experiencing God's liberating grace. Kingdom agents love people too much to be cowards. They are loving but not tolerant of obstacles to faith in Christ. If we care about every man, woman, and child in our communities, we will be patient with their sin but confront idolatry. People can come to Jesus with sin in their lives, with their arms open wide. But an idol is given a place only Jesus can fill, leaving people forced to choose: Jesus or idols.

For even though idolatry may sound so three thousand years ago, the reason it remains the most talked-about sin in Scripture is not merely because the worship of stone, silver, and wooden images was so prevalent in those days. The reason the Bible warns us so consistently about the dangers of idolatry is because God knows they still have deep designs on our hearts. Yours and mine. Right this minute.

All of our behaviors—both our obedience and our sin—stem from the object (or objects) 'of our worship. This truth helps us see God's amazing wisdom in how he ordered his Ten Commandments, choosing to begin, of course, with this mandate: "Thou shalt have no other gods before me" (Exod. 20:3 KJV). Martin Luther, writing in his commentary on this section of Scripture, said, "Where the heart is rightly disposed toward God, and this commandment is observed, all the others follow." In other words, a person cannot break Commandments Two through Ten without first breaking Commandment One. Our obedience to God in *practical* matters flows from our unadulterated worship of him as a *central* matter.

Life in the kingdom requires unrivaled loyalty to the King.

Paul was able to put skin on this truth by sharing his observations of the church in Thessalonica, noting how they had "turned to God from idols to serve the living and true God" (1 Thess. 1:9). Their conversion to Christ—their supernatural transfer from the kingdom of darkness to the kingdom of light—had accomplished in them what conversion was designed to do, the same thing it's designed to do in all of us: *a complete change of loyalty* from the old life to the new. They had locked down their loyalties on God's radio frequency and torn off the knob. They had put all their eggs in his basket and told all other suitors to take a hike.

And just look what this sweeping transformation had caused to happen in their lives. Paul praised these early believers for their "work of faith, labor of love, and endurance of hope in our Lord Jesus Christ" (v. 3). They were performing the hard work of the kingdom with a noticeable vigor of zeal, joy, and confidence—all those things we Christians want to do but often *can't* do because our hearts have so many ventricles bleeding off in other directions.

This complete turning away from their idols and toward their God is what made this early church able to live out a kingdom-shaped life. For by virtue of this new focus and freedom, not only were they able to stay busy on subversive mission, God's Word says they were watching and waiting "for His Son from heaven, whom He raised from the dead—Jesus, who rescues us from the coming wrath" (v. 10).

They were truly experiencing the "already, but not yet."

Sounds exciting, doesn't it?

Well, that's what can happen when we stop dragging these idols around all day and bringing them back home with us at night, when we realize that all they offer us is the "ignorance" of dividing our loyalties (Acts 17:29–30) and an "empty way of life" in return for all their fancy promises about filling us up (1 Pet. 1:18).

Break it all down, and idolatry is what hangs us up. It is the drain at the heart of our kingdom weakness.

Tertullian, an early church father from the second century who is remembered as perhaps the most prolific author of his generation, spoke to this matter:

The principle crime of the human race is idolatry. For although each single fault retains its own proper feature, although it is destined to judgment under its own proper name, yet it is marked off under the general [heading] of idolatry. Set aside names, examine works, and the idolater is likewise a murderer. . . . Thus it comes to pass that in idolatry all crimes are detected, and in all crimes idolatry.[2]

So when the Bible speaks of idolatry, God is referring to *anything* we allow to occupy the place of King Jesus in our values, priorities, and emotions. Those "anythings" are what rob us of our subversive qualities.

According to pastor Tim Keller, these idols of ours tend to orient themselves around three broad categories: personal, religious, and cultural.

- *Personal idols* are those desires and temptations that individuals commonly pursue: greed, sex, power, various forms of personal indulgence and expression.
- *Religious idols* are those beliefs and practices we employ to quiet our fears and invite inner comfort without having to resort to dependent devotion toward God.
- *Cultural idols* present themselves whenever we pursue our hopes and ambitions through the deceptive promises of our world's ideologies and values.[3]

But beyond these usual, sinful suspects that highlight the idolatry catalog—our wasteful habits, our selfish demands, our secret escapes—we are more than capable of turning even *good* things into god things. Everything from church involvement, to home maintenance, to extended family obligations, to a host of other worthwhile endeavors—any of these can become tyrants we allow to dominate and control us, activities that do more for our self-image and unmet emotional needs than for our pure pursuit of Christ's kingdom mission.

We can make idols of our *children*, for example, based on a warped view of why God gives us children in the first place, eventually causing spiritual harm to both our kids, our spouses, and ourselves. When we worship our children, we pervert the mission of God explained in Malachi: "Didn't the one God make us with a remnant of His life-breath? And what does the One seek? A godly offspring. So watch yourselves carefully, and do not act treacherously against the wife of your youth" (Mal. 2:15).

We can make an idol of our *work,* overdoing a noble, God-ordained responsibility until it commands far too much of our time and attention, constantly winning the tug-of-war for our first loyalty. Again, we pervert the intention of God by taking our platform for his glory and influence (our jobs) and becoming like every other employee in the world. A person can gain the whole world through 24/7 commitment to the job but lose his or her own soul and family in the process.

Success can become a similar goddess of sorts, as philosopher William James wrote about in the early 1900s (using a term stronger than "goddess" to describe it), to which we are willing to sacrifice our health and relationships in order to achieve a seductive taste of financial prosperity. *Exercise and recreation* can become an idol if we allow our weeknight and weekend hobbies to occupy inordinate amounts of our effort, thinking, and planning. *Technology*, too, can become an idol if we become so drawn to and dependent on its capabilities that we refuse ever to quiet or align ourselves to the rhythms of life with God.

So as it turns out, idols from tribal Asia are no sillier and potentially sinister than idols from Wal-Mart. The Baals and Ashteroths of ancient times may perhaps be today's overpriced season tickets to our favorite sports teams, activities, and events. At least be willing to consider it.

The church, too, can set up idols right there in their meeting areas. People make idols of a certain kind of worship style, letting it carry more clout in their minds than other, more valuable elements and aspects of life in the kingdom. People make idols of church leaders and authority figures, ascribing more allegiance to their words and perspectives than to God himself. Some people grow overly attached to ministry methods that may have been effective and appropriate during a certain season or situation in the past, finding themselves resistant to what the Lord is wanting to accomplish through his people at this moment in time.

One obvious idol of the church is the church itself. More than methodological arrogance, a church-centric mind-set exists that damages the mission of God and its substantive impact in a community. Church-centric people not only look down on the "heathens" in the community who hang out in bars and don't attend their church, but they pity other Christians who attend church in the wrong location or denomination (not theirs, of course). Jesus demands and deserves our worship and is jealous when bricks, mortar, and locations become objects of worship.

My friend Reggie McNeal describes this church idolatry in another way. The advancement of the kingdom is hindered when church-centric people believe their physical location is the ultimate *destination* for everyone in their community. They establish church scorecards to reflect that belief. Although historically we say nickels, noses, and sometimes baptisms are most important, these can sometimes give way to a noses-only mentality. More is better, no matter who "more" might be. Our communities can go to hell as long as our churches are full of people. The influence is felt in churches from one hundred to ten thousand in attendance. Those beliefs shift dramatically in the subversive kingdom. McNeal said:

> When the church thinks it's the destination, it also confuses the scorecard. It thinks that if people are hovering around and in the church, the church is winning. The truth is, when that's the case, the church is really keeping people from where they want to go, from their real destination. The destination is life. . . . Abundant life is lived out with loved ones, friends, and acquaintances in the marketplace, in the home, in the neighborhood, in the world.[4]

The local church was born in the heart of God but is a tool that consists of missionaries being deployed in the community to seek and save the lost. The church is a genius invention by God and a marvelous tool when under the lordship of Christ. God intended the local church to worship, but never did he intend for the local church to become an object of worship. *That is idolatry,* and it exists in every community in America.

So the great reformer John Calvin couldn't have been more accurate in referring to the human heart and mind as a "perpetual factory of idols." If we run through the supply we have on hand, we can always make more. And because we sacrifice so much *for* them and invest so much *in* them, we fight hard when we're called to separate ourselves *from* them.

But we *must* separate ourselves from them.

And that means first recognizing that we *have* them, that their pull on us is strong and sentimental, and that falling for their convincing lines is so easy. We are now being tempted—and will *always* be tempted—to rejoin the world's rebellion against God, to consider him one among many, to continue our love affair with "something created instead of the Creator, who is praised forever" (Rom. 1:25). When we desire any object, experience, status, or emotion more than we desire our King, we are living out of line with our kingdom purpose.

This will not go well.

This will not end well.

But there is a way to *get* well.

That "way" is through worship.

Worship

New life in the kingdom of Christ involves a change in our worship. To repeat Paul's words, it requires a "turn[ing] to God from idols to serve the living and true God." To say it another way, we don't so much hammer our idols into dusty oblivion as we choke out their oxygen supply by filling our hearts so full of Jesus.

The meaning of "to serve" in this biblical context actually has more to do with *worshipping* than *working*. It doesn't mean just getting busy doing things for God. The accent is on possessing such a deep, pure, unmixed devotion to the Lord that serving him becomes the logical result of our allegiance. By focusing so directly on him and his glory, our grateful response is to begin doing whatever pleases him.

So as we learn to worship God, the kingdom of God becomes more evident in our lives. We find the spark and motivation to rebel against the world's rebellion and to leave our cherished idols in the dust. We realize through our worship of the one true God that he is, well . . . the *one true God.*

And our idols don't easily survive in such an environment.

Near the end of the last century, the church witnessed what can appropriately be called a worldwide reemphasis on worship. Largely led by musicians who seemed to recognize that the tone of worship among the body of Christ had become somewhat stale, repetitive, and perhaps even a bit self-gratifying, this movement challenged us toward an ethic of worship that goes beyond just singing the songs— worship that translates into responsive action, motivating us into forward kingdom motion. From places like Hillsong in Australia, with Matt Redmond and Delirious in England, on to the United States and the Passion movement—among others—young adults (primarily) caught a fresh vision for what worship was all about. While some critics looked for fault among those involved or in the theology of their song lyrics, it's safe to say that many of those who prefer traditional styles of music and singing were forced to rethink the purpose of Christian worship. Ultimately people all over the world, both in customary and contemporary church settings, deepened both their understanding and experience of what it means to worship in spirit and truth.

I personally believe, in fact, that what we are seeing today among God's people as a more passionate, deliberate confrontation of human need and injustice has been triggered—at least in part—by people responding to his leading through a new heart for worship. Real, genuine worship leads to a kingdom lifestyle.

I think of the Church at Brook Hills in Birmingham, Alabama, which has developed a compassionate heart for the hurting and needy in many parts of the world, as well in their own county and context. When pastor David Platt discovered from their local Department of Human Resources that the current needs of all the children awaiting adoption or foster care in their area could be met by 150 available families, *160* families in their church committed to exploring the possibilities. The idol of complacency and the world's expectation of family proved unworthy gods as believers saw a kingdom opportunity in front of them. "We are discovering the indescribable joy of sacrificial love for others," Platt said, "and along the way we are learning more about the inexpressible wonder of God's sacrificial love for us."[5] To use their term, they "rebelled" against the American dream. Indeed.

Only an authentic kind of worship can cause that.

I think of the Summit Church in Durham, North Carolina, which felt led of God to focus hard on five key avenues of ministry: the homeless, orphans and foster children, prisoners, unwed mothers and widows, as well as high school dropouts and at-risk students. Citing the inspiration of Psalm 68:5–6, which reveals God as the "father of the fatherless and a champion of widows," One who "provides homes for those who are deserted" and "leads out the prisoners to prosperity," they asked themselves what would happen if they went out consistently into their surrounding areas, putting the love of Christ on display through both word and deed. "It is our prayer that our community will be radically transformed by the gospel," they say, "as we allow Him to radically transform us." The idols that make such outreaches seem too hard, too expensive, too risky, or too inconvenient were no match for this church's devotion to the one true God.[6]

Only an authentic kind of worship can cause that.

I think of a thirty-member Westlake, California, church called the Filling Station, which had slowly collected $75,000 over several years to advance their dream of building a permanent structure to meet in. But when they heard about a struggling church in southern Sudan whose building had twice been destroyed during that country's lengthy civil war, they believed God was leading them to divert the full amount of their special building fund toward the project. The feeling among the membership was unanimous. And today the Filling Station enjoys a relationship with a sister church a world away, all because they didn't let money and ambition become an idol that kept them from being part of God's kingdom calling. In fact, "we'd love to do more," says pastor Steve Ridinger. "To God be the glory. We're just following along."[7]

The Old Testament teaches that the active demonstration of our heart for the poor elicits his protective blessing and favor on our lives (Ps. 41:1–3, among others), while our hardness and indifference toward others in need causes him to close his ears to our inconsistent, hypocritical, two-faced worship (Isa. 58:1–4). Jesus, of course, in the continuation of his kingdom teaching in Matthew 25, said that our refusal to help those in desperate need—the hungry, the thirsty, the stranger, the naked, the prisoner—will erect a barrier to receiving his approval on Judgment Day.

Our most deceptive, distracting idols will start to fall away as we yield ourselves wholeheartedly to God in worship. And at the same time, our desire to cooperate with him on kingdom business in the streets, homes, neighborhoods, and nations of the world will spike as a result.

Spirit-and-truth worship is an idol killer.

Inside Out

As we begin making the turn in this book from looking at our kingdom selves to looking at our kingdom communities, let's realize that the purpose of slaying our idols is not merely to keep their depressing end results from running roughshod over our lives. The greater purpose—the true kingdom purpose—behind eliminating these drains on our joy and effectiveness is to make us more aware and available for God's work of destroying idols in the population at large. How exciting would it be to get past the slogging process of dealing with our own junk so we can be more readily useful to him in subverting the hostage-producing tactics of our enemy?

That's where we're going with all this.

But for this we need one another.

"There is no limit to the idolatries the human heart can manufacture," writes Trevin Wax in his book *Holy Subversion*. "We must, as churches, think through ways that we can undermine the idols before a watching world. Our goal must be to identify the prevailing idolatries of our culture and then to deliberately subvert them."[8]

Yes, there is much of value in dealing with the personal subjects we've been addressing. Our integrity and interactions as individuals can go a long way in showing others the power of our King to transform lives. But even though some of our subverting work can (and will) be accomplished one-on-one—just you and I out there, on daily mission—the best work of God's people happens among groups, classes, and friends from within the entire church body, multiplying our kingdom potential through our shared lives as subversives.

So thinking back through what we've been examining in these last few chapters, let's not only work at putting our own "talents" to use, but also the resources God has given us to invest in whatever subversive activity we can think of.

Let's do it together.

May we not only allow the Lord to change our ways of acting, our ways of responding, our ways of entertaining ourselves, our ways of navigating the gray areas with truth and honesty.

Let's hold one another accountable for integrity.

May we not only be willing to go the extra mile for our own neighbors and family, our coworkers and contacts, our friends and even our enemies.

Let's dream up proactive ways we can care for people together.

May we become so pure and unadulterated in our personal level of worship that our old familiar idols start thinking of us as strangers. And better yet . . .

Let's lead others to this place of freedom as well.

Together.

There are too many people today who are in bondage to the world's fallen system, whose lives are guided by philosophies and thinking patterns that offer them no hope for anything other than ultimate death and despair. Truly the world rages in full-blown rebellion against the rightful reign of our King. And though there may not be as many of us as we'd like, and though we may not all agree on how God wants it done, he has chosen a people to man the outposts of his kingdom. He has come near geographically, not just chronologically. As witnesses to the in-breaking of his kingdom in our own lives, we are part of God's agenda to push back the lostness and brokenness of the world.

Your part is big. But *our* part is bigger.

So look around. See who's with you—your fellow rebels,

each having "turned to God from idols to serve the living and true God."

Your kingdom self is a kingdom army.

PART III

A Subversive Plan of Action

8

The King's Mission

A few years ago my kids fell in love with "Bob the Builder." His chant was catchy and simple: "Can we fix it? Yes, we can." So we all believed.

We all have a mission—from Bob the Builder to Bob the Barber. Everyone has something that gets them up in the morning or wakes them in the middle of the night. Everybody is living a "purpose-driven life" (in respect to my friend Rick Warren and one of the best-selling books in history). From video games to working with AIDS victims in Ethiopia, to college football or working in the local homeless shelter, people are designed to find purpose—and they do. Some even choose to live for the purpose of nothing! But in reality, that in itself is a purpose. I am saddened by the trivial things that drive life for many people. But I am even more saddened by how easily I myself can get distracted from the mission of God to pursue other, less important purposes.

Two critical questions should follow your initial embrace of kingdom citizenship. The first question is, *What is the King's mission?* Now don't zoom past this first one too quickly. You may think it's a no-brainer, but if you really want to be a significant part of the King's mission, you must go beyond knowing the right answer, praying, and giving money to world mission efforts.

The second question is equally important: *What is my role in the King's mission?* Again, another no-brainer, it seems. But on second glance, wrong or shallow answers to these questions can get to the heart of our ineptness on the King's mission.

Often our first and only question is, *What can I possibly contribute to the King's mission?* What could be wrong with such a question? Look closely, and you find it is often rooted in the desire to *contribute* versus a desire to fully *embrace* the King's mission with complete abandonment. This conservative approach usually leads to typical Christian decisions to give ten percent (or less) to your church, help out with the children's ministry, or maybe even go on an international mission trip every few years. I call it the donation level. You may feel better about yourself, but you have missed the incredible adventure of being on 24/7 mission for the King.

Where should you start to find the answers to my first two questions? Go on a serious journey of prayer and study in order to let God shape your heart and life around his mission. Study Jesus' work on earth and watch him in action. But also listen to Jesus interpret life through the eyes of his mission for the world.

For example, after his incredible, life-changing meeting with the hated tax collector Zacchaeus, Jesus reviewed his purpose-driven life for everyone to hear. All had been witness to the tangible example of Jesus' purpose, fulfilled in the least likely of people—Zacchaeus. And that mission, Jesus said, could be summarized this way: "The Son of Man has come to seek and to save the lost" (Luke 19:10). That is the King's mission. But look for different perspectives from his life as you read Scripture. Journal and pray through how the life of Jesus was shaped. Then let the King shape your heart around what it means to invest your all in his mission, not just whatever you can give.

David and Heidi Baniszewski asked the right questions about the King's mission and came to some radical conclusions as a result. They moved from Indianapolis to Rock Hill, South Carolina, for David to become principal of a private Christian school. Moving from a big city in the North to a small town in the South, warmer climate and all, seemed like the right thing to do at David and Heidi's station in life. But what they did next was not a natural, reflex reaction. They bought a rundown house on the most dangerous street in Rock Hill and named it the Dream Center. Paul and Barbara Crosby made a similar move from a beautiful condominium on Lake Wylie to a street near David and Heidi.

They now do ministry together and lead North Rock Hill Church to do the same. From youth, to single parents, to the elderly, all know that the Dream Center is there for them.

People on the margins are no longer on the margins—at least on those streets. Everybody in the blocks surrounding the Dream Center hears the life-changing story of Jesus through word and deed.

The right questions about the King's mission will lead to radical answers.

What is the King's mission?

What is my role in the King's mission?

Consider them if you dare.

A Study in Contrasts

The dominant, culture-shaping story throughout much of the world for the past three hundred years has been the pursuit of *progress*—a story inspired by the hope that humanity, by maximizing its powers of intellect, discovery, and initiative, is fully capable of creating its own version of heaven on earth.

The late missionary/theologian Lesslie Newbigin traced this story back to the new governments that were established in the afterglow of the French and American revolutions. He noted that many of the tenets behind these cultural movements were developed during the age of Enlightenment, later to be embodied in such heady texts as Thomas Paine's *The Rights of Man*, and further articulated in FDR's "Four Freedoms" speech before the U.S. Congress in 1941—as well as "in the promises which any political party must now make if it is to have a hope of power."[1]

And while I'll leave it to others more skilled than I to evaluate the political implications of such analysis, I do know that the challenge of the *church* in our age is to live, function, and minister within a culture that demands few if any limits on its personal freedoms, one which has embraced consumerism as a way of life, one which attempts to use what it has—its own inner drive and resources—to get what it wants. That's the kind of thinking and energy that turns on the coffeepot each morning in most homes throughout the Western world. This is the generational mind-set embedded into the fabric of modern life and the expectations of modern man.

Try harder.

Work smarter.

Take charge.

Make it happen.

But what is foundationally wrong with this picture?

The problem is that the Bible—our authority on all life and our guide to all truth—doesn't subscribe to this same story of human progress. The story of the Bible (and, therefore, the story we as Christians are called to tell and participate in) is the story of human *redemption*.

Progress. Redemption.

Big difference.

The first one futilely attempts to fashion heaven on earth in the form of hard work, positive energy, peaceful thoughts, better nutrition, and stuff like that. The other successfully brings heaven *to* earth in the form of God's Son and his atoning death, sent here to redeem (to "buy back") the captives of this oppressive world order and to set them free. One fails; the other *cannot* fail. People don't move toward a paradisiacal "not yet" by being turned loose to pursue their own personally beneficial ends. The only "not yet" that promises any joy and freedom is the "not yet" of Christ's consummated kingdom. And none of us *progresses* toward it; we are *redeemed into it*.

Life enslaves. But Jesus saves.

Not too long ago I had the opportunity to speak to the Religion Newswriters Association at the *Washington Post* building in Washington, DC. It gave me the chance to share with secular religion reporters from across the United States what our current research is telling us about the beliefs and practices of evangelicals today. But it doesn't take a research professional to interpret what I observed among this cross-section of journalists gathered that day in such a distinguished setting. When one of the other speakers at the event—a reporter himself—responded to a question about world religions by declaring, "I believe Jesus is the only way to God," more than a few folks looked uncomfortable. To the people in that room (and to most people, really), making such a bold, restrictive claim smacked of exclusivism, narrow-mindedness, and intolerance, a real misunderstanding of wider thought. The assertion of a "narrow" way—salvation through Jesus Christ alone—was (and always is) offensive to normal folks. But it is essential to us.

And yet isn't the "broad" way of human progress littered with the corpses of those who tried and failed to achieve what they hoped to accomplish? Despite all these years of concerted effort, what kind of news and business headlines continue to float to the top of the public consciousness on most days of the week? By pursuing their own paths and pleasures in ways that cut God out of the picture—at least in any fashion beyond the sentimental, religiously controlled version of spiritual practice—the search for "heaven on earth" fails to accomplish even its own admitted goals, often in miserably lonely and discouraging detail.

So here's just the way it is (with apologies to Thomas Paine): The story of human progress is 100 percent guaranteed to have a bad ending, no matter how many variations people come up with, no matter how many different ways they try to spin things. Christ alone and his work of redeeming helpless humankind is the sole remedy for what ails the inhabitants of any society, in any age, in any place.

There is only one way. The narrow way.

But (and here's where we start to see our kingdom role in all this) it's not so narrow that it can't handle more travelers.

As we begin wrapping our arms around the call to action that Christ extends to his kingdom agents, we must not fail to see the primary importance of the *gospel* in framing our plan of subversive attack. Redemption is a reality we must not be ashamed of, even in a world that beats its boot-straps to the tune of human potential and progress. Christ's redemption is the great hope—the only hope—for the culture we live in. The only thing "progress" does is make excuses for the bondage.

Here is reality at ground level: People who have been deceived into thinking they can successfully map the course of their own destiny, people who are wearing themselves out trying to cobble together a life that's too big to be figured out on their own, people whose greatest need isn't for more money or better job prospects or a couple of lucky breaks—they need Jesus.

Just like we needed Jesus—and *still* need Jesus.

But this divine turn of events that we recognize as the *gospel*—God in Christ reaching down to the broken and lost world, rescuing them from bondage, and transferring them into God's kingdom of light—is actually even more than that. The gospel is not merely the story of the Bible and the only hope for hopeless mankind. It is indeed the grandest expression of God's *mission*.

And God's mission needs to be *our* mission.

God's Mission, Our Mission

Yes, God has a mission.

In many ways it wouldn't really matter *what* his mission is. If it is God's mission, then it outranks whatever other mission we've decided we want to build our lives around as Christian believers. If it is God's mission, then it should define what his redeemed people are more concerned about than anything else. If it is God's mission, then it should also be the church's mission. It should orient our schedule and priorities. It should dictate our activities and why we do them.

Because actually, the church doesn't *have* a mission; the mission has a *church*. God, who by nature is on purpose and on task, has invited people like us, gathered in churches like ours, to join him in fulfilling his chief desire.

And that mission is this: *for God to be glorified.*

"The heavens," for example, "declare the glory of God"

(Ps. 19:1). He has done this on purpose, Scripture says. The beauty and precision of nature work together to advance his stated goal. He has deliberately fashioned the world so it manifests his glory and gives ample, visible evidence of his power, wisdom, and grandeur.

But something happened on the heels of creation and at the center of paradise. Sin entered the hearts of God's image bearers. The fabric of God's good creation was stained and torn. Men no longer desired God's presence; they hid from him. Relationships at every turn were affected. Between God and humanity. Between man and woman. Between brothers. And this story continues for all of history.

To restore God's perfect place for creation, the wonders of creation weren't enough. So God selected a historic moment in time to send his only Son to walk the earth in human flesh, to reveal himself and his goodness to creation (John 1:8). This Son came to establish a kingdom and redeem a people. And knowing that mankind would naturally reject this humble, loving initiative on his part, God chose the perfect vehicles of Christ's death and resurrection to redeem fallen sinners through his "glorious grace" so that we who put our hope in him "might bring praise to His glory" (Eph. 1:6, 12). God is known ultimately by his glory being revealed in the face of the crucified and resurrected Jesus Christ (2 Cor. 4:6). His kingdom expands through the salvation of people (Col. 1:14–15).

God's mission is God's glory.

He is creating a kingdom *for his glory.*

He saves people through the gospel *for his glory.*

His purposes will all be accomplished *for his glory.*

And so he has placed us here in the church for one reason: to participate in his mission.

To bring him glory.

So for us to be invested in declaring the gospel is not just the memorization of bullet points and Bible verses. It's not the development of a hunter's mentality, seeing how many people we can witness to in a given period. It is so much bigger and more all-encompassing than that. What we do in living, breathing, sharing, and demonstrating the gospel of Jesus Christ—in a wide and ever-growing number of ways—*we do for his glory.* That's it. This is your purpose and mine every day of the week. To bring him glory. That is God's mission.

And because it is his, it is ours as well.

And because it is ours, we perform it through his church.

The Church on Mission

Some people talk as if the church isn't necessary to this endeavor anymore, that it no longer applies to his plan and mission to the same degree it once did. They say, "God is at work outside the church"—*and, yes, he is.* They say, "The kingdom is bigger than the church"—*and, yes, it is.* They say, "The kingdom of God is not the church"—*and no, it isn't.*

But the missionary purpose that forges our identity, placed within us by a missional God, continues to draw us into the core of his kingdom activity. The ministry of his gospel has been designed "so that God's multi-faceted wisdom may now be made known *through the church"* (Eph. 3:10, italics added). And so that through us, he receives glory.

The church, therefore, remains his central tool for accomplishing the subversive kingdom's agenda. No, we are not the means of reconciliation any more than the misinformed modern citizen is the potential conduit to heaven on earth. God does the saving, not the church. But just as he sent Jesus here to establish a beachhead for the kingdom, and just as Jesus dispatched his first disciples to carry out his kingdom plan (John 20:21), the church has now emerged in the wake of this mission, called to advance God's kingdom by taking gospel light into the darkest corners of society as his messengers. Not to prove we're right. Not to win. Not because we're better than everybody else. We go because we are carrying out the mission of our founder. We go because we are sent by him, and he sends us empowered by his Spirit.

And "go" is the right word for how we do it.

When Christ instructed his followers to head out under the Holy Spirit's direction and empowering, bearing witness of him "in Jerusalem, in all Judea and Samaria, and to the ends of the earth" (Acts 1:8), this signaled a new chapter in kingdom work. No longer were God's people to be continually drawn *toward* Jerusalem, as had been the case throughout the Old Testament. They were now being sent out *from* Jerusalem. The *centripetal* mission of bringing outsiders into an earthly city was being replaced by the *centrifugal* mission of taking heaven's glories to the cities of the world. The indwelling Holy Spirit and his amazing visitation at the Pentecost celebration of Acts 2 meant the church was being empowered to pursue, not to be pursued.

This is why, when giving a talk at a missions meeting recently, I said rather facetiously, since it was a non-Pentecostal gathering, "What we need in our churches—in all kinds of churches—is more speaking in tongues." (Insert nervous laughter here.) My focus—and what each of us along all points of the Christian spectrum should be able to concur with—is this: the church needs to be speaking the heart languages of all the world's people groups, both at home and abroad. Rather than merely throwing open the doors of our building to a "come and see" festivity (and thereby considering ourselves fully compliant with a kingdom calling), we need to be going out into the darkness with a "here's light" message of freedom for all kinds of people, in all sorts of life settings and situations.

So I say any church daring to call itself *missional* might consider doing three kingdom things: (1) serving locally, (2) planting nationally, and (3) adopting an unreached people group globally. Why? Because God wants his glory to be manifest before men and women everywhere through his covenant people on earth. He wants his *found* children wholeheartedly engaged in rescuing his *lost* children. He wants his people living and declaring his grace to those who are starting to see the pointlessness of human progress.

What they need is redemption. And because they exist in every town, county, state, and nation of the world, that's where his church is commissioned to go.

This is what motivated Archbishop Bob Duncan to call

for a thousand new Anglican congregations and communities of faith to be planted in North America, a primary strategy for reaching the continent with the good news of the gospel. When I spoke at the first national gathering of the Anglican 1000 initiative, I noticed the attendees did not look quite like the people who show up at my typical church planting sessions. These folks wore purple shirts and clerical collars. Many of them wore robes (or as my kids refer to it, "a dress")—not the type of apparel I customarily see at my denomination's annual meeting. Nor was it the comfortable jeans and untucked shirt I usually wear when I'm speaking. Nevertheless, we were gathered together as one in Plano, Texas, to discuss ideas that would help them reach their goal of planting a thousand new churches in the coming years. God's glory and the unity among his kingdom subversives are big enough for us to do that.

Today this strategy is turning up unsaved soil through people like Mark Riggs and Jonathan Kuehling, who are planting Living Water Anglican Church in Florence, South Carolina. It's happening through Matthew Pechanio and the newly planted Church of the Ascension in Elmhurst, Illinois. It's happening through Barclay Mayo and the Mountain Valley Mission in Squamish, British Columbia, where they are connecting people to the love and forgiveness of Jesus through such means as establishing a food co-op and teaching a Christian apologetics class at a local coffee shop. Scores of these churches are popping up across the North American landscape, taking the gospel into their communities both by proclaiming it and personifying it. They are on mission.

The church, as it turns out, only exists because God is *missional.* He is a "sender" as part of his nature. So if the church is going to function the way it's supposed to, we need to condition ourselves to live "sent lives." Jesus was sent to establish his kingdom. As kingdom citizens, we live *sent.* We must realize that for subversive transformation to take place, it must happen not only in times of gathered worship but through a whole week's worth of kingdom-oriented living and going. Culture expects us to be all about our Sunday morning huddles, but when we live beyond the safe and warm huddle, our lives become an argument against their perception of us.

Jesus said, for example, that he came "to seek and to save the lost" (Luke 19:10). If we as the church are going to own our calling as messengers of his salvation, then we need to join him on rescue mission, knowing we cannot fulfill this mandate simply by getting together on Sunday morning, teaching our best Bible studies, singing our best songs, and preaching our best sermons. Yes, those things are important. Key. Valuable. But a church that cannot locate its pulse for entering the culture to engage the lost and see them reconciled with their Father is not bringing him the full glory he desires and deserves.

Jesus also said that he came to "preach good news to the poor . . . to proclaim freedom to the captives and recovery of sight to the blind, to set free the oppressed" (Luke 4:18), to serve the helpless and hurting. Therefore, we as the church need to join him in going to the mistreated and marginalized, restoring a sense of justice to these situations that will one day be made completely right in his consummated kingdom. In this way we introduce small, tangible doses of "already" into the still unseen "not yet." Like a recent commercial says, produced by the United Methodist Church to describe their work in disaster relief, "Sometimes prayer brings miracles. Other times it brings heavy machinery." When the church scatters to do its kingdom work, lives are transformed in the process, both physically and spiritually.

It's the essence of our subversive agenda.

This is what motivated churches like Ginghamsburg Church near Dayton, Ohio, to increase ministry efforts aimed at counteracting the loss of thirty-three thousand manufacturing jobs in their hometown over an eight-year period. Median income had dropped more than 10 percent, and the poverty rate among school-age children showed a corresponding spike. Today they're part of donating thousands of dollars worth of food and essentials to area families through the ClipShopShare couponing program. A ministry they call New Path, a 501(c)(3) outreach arm, serves thousands more in surrounding communities through gifts of clothing, furniture, cars, medical equipment, pet care, GED classes, lunches for seniors, and similar efforts, growing more imaginative and effective all the time. They've adopted a public elementary school where they volunteer as teacher aides and perform numerous other duties to ease the school's financial burdens while also opening doors for impacting a new generation. I could name more.

Internationally, for example, they and their partner churches have contributed more than $5 million toward relief efforts in the impoverished Darfur region of Sudan, investing in agriculture, child protection, and safe water projects. They are spearheading dozens of mission teams and opportunities year-round, from continued hurricane relief efforts in New Orleans (seventy so far) to local Project Neighborhood service days, as well as out-of-country trips to Africa, South America, and other locales, bringing medical care, construction expertise, and spiritual encouragement to some of the neediest places on earth.

As pastor Mike Slaughter says, "If the world is ever going to take the good news seriously, then we must repent and realign our priorities and resources with the message and mission of Jesus. Religion that honors God is religion with feet."[2]

This is why it's so important that the church not cave to a consumerist mentality, becoming a mere dispenser of religious goods and services, turning itself into little more than a "way station" where people come to get what they think they need, purchased with minimal offerings of time and money. We are not here to provide a hub of community-center activity unhinged from true, kingdom mission. A church that becomes activity-driven rather than kingdom-driven runs the risk of ceasing to be an authentic church at all because it is no longer focused on bringing God's glory to its neighborhood and the nations. The glorious, redeeming gospel of Jesus Christ, living and operating and generously shared through his church, is not just what we've been sent here to offer whenever people bother to show up. It's what we've been *sent out* from here to give.

Keep the ideas of this chapter firmly in mind, for they are the heartbeat of our marching orders as kingdom agents.

Our subversive plan of action is to live for God's *glory*, which is most vividly expressed in the sharing and receiving of the *gospel*, which is most powerfully administered through the *church*—people who have been set free by God from the results of sin and death to become part of his plan for setting others free as well.

Return to Glory

In order for the church to recover its missional passion, we must reclaim our lost sense of the awesome, overarching glory of God's mission. Most Christians do not deny the orthodox doctrines of Scripture. We grasp the fact that God has revealed himself to us as Lord and King. But to borrow the words of author David Wells, the modern church has been "caged" by a diminishing of who God really is.

> We have turned to a God we can use rather than a God we must obey; we have turned to a God who will fulfill our need rather than a God before whom we must surrender our rights to ourselves. He is a God for us, for our satisfaction—not because we have learned to think of him in this way through Christ but because we have learned to think of him this way through the marketplace. Everything is for us, for our pleasure, for our satisfaction, and we have come to assume that it must be so in the church as well.[3]

We have shrunk God down to our size. We have limited the scope of his mission in our minds. We have unwittingly bought into the idea that progress is more important than redemption.

And this is chiefly why our zeal for evangelism and the gospel has been undermined—not because we don't care, not because we don't know what to do. We have simply replaced God's purpose for the world with our own purpose for the world. Even when we serve and help and give and share, we too often do it from a sense of obligation or a desire to impress. We have become a church steered by many different motivations but all too rarely by a singular desire to glorify God. Wells is right: "We will not be able to recover the vision and understanding of God's grandeur until we recover an understanding of ourselves as creatures who have been made to know such grandeur."[4]

The message that emanates from the life and work of the apostle Paul, who was without argument the most productive missionary in the history of the church, is that we cannot hope to be either faithful or effective in kingdom service while being overly concerned about our own needs.

On two occasions he called himself an "ambassador." That's a pretty important job. Where I grew up in New York, those were the people who didn't have to pay parking tickets. They mattered. And Paul said, "We are ambassadors for Christ" (2 Cor. 5:20). Yet the only other time we read him referring to himself by that title, he said he was an "ambassador in chains" (Eph. 6:20). Yes, he was an ambassador—just as we are—yet that ambassadorial role, representing King Jesus, did not mean Paul was without hardship.

No one survives the harsh, abusive treatment he endured

without living for something bigger than himself. We might assume, then, Paul was simply that devoted to the people he was called to serve. His compassion for them, his selfless interest in them, his desire that they experience the fruit of the gospel—all of these must have come together to make him an unstoppable force.

Well, yes, Paul was devoted to the churches and the people who comprised them. He possessed an uncommon zeal to see others convinced of gospel truth and redeemed through God's eternal mercy and grace. But it wasn't concern for his neighbors that ultimately motivated Paul to such extremes of spiritual exertion and sacrifice. It was Jesus' love that "compelled" him (2 Cor. 5:14). "To live is Christ," he said (Phil. 1:21).

And we, too—if we wish to be faithful to our calling—must live supremely for the glory of God and what he is doing through his Son in our world.

If we are not on this mission, then we must ask ourselves what we're doing here. Are we just working to make the church a more acceptable place to our friends and neighbors? Are we looking for a nice place to socialize on Wednesday nights? Are we turning spiritual cranks and pulleys because we think the church is supposed to do those things, because we feel better about ourselves when we do them?

The only thing that really matters is this: our God has a mission. That's why he sent Jesus here on subversive terms. And that's why he established the church—churches like yours and churches like mine—to join him on mission to reestablish his glory over all creation.

This is why God has given his church the "keys of the

kingdom of heaven," so that "whatever you bind on earth is already bound in heaven, and whatever you loose on earth is already loosed in heaven" (Matt. 16:19). To people in the world who live chained to the notion that their desired ambitions can be achieved on earth, the church possesses their liberating answer. They are no longer forced to exist in the bondage of living from experience to experience. For some this "bondage" takes the form of workout gyms, corner offices, organic food stores, and all the apparent trappings of success. But for others it means gambling losses, broken relationships, wasted opportunities, prescription drug abuse. For many it's a roller-coaster mix between the two, a frantic navigation of highs and lows. And for all it's a life that leads *away* from ultimate purpose and permanence.

Through the gospel those individuals who are "bound" in spiritual darkness can be "loosed" from what has held them captive—*redeemed* from their slavery. God's plan for overthrowing the devil's dominion, freeing its hostages, and advancing Christ's kingdom is for the church to proclaim the good news of Jesus Christ in both word and deed. That's how he pursues his plan of bringing all creation under his authority and deriving glory for himself in the process.

May this be the purpose behind all our subversion.

When we grasp the enormity of this calling and our role within it, we will begin trusting the Spirit to empower us to engage the lost, serve the hurting, and live "sent lives" as Christian believers united in kingdom purpose. We will live out the difference that Jesus makes in our hearts not because people expect it but because it shows what our God can accomplish. We will talk with others about the power of the gospel not just because they're lost but because our Lord and King is glorified in finding them.

Begin your plan of action there, and get ready to see what happens around you when *God* starts making progress.

9

A Sign of Things to Come

When we started our first church—a fledgling congregation in the inner city of Buffalo, New York—it was not a pretty sight. I've mentioned earlier that it was in a bad part of town, nowhere near where the "beautiful people" lived, the kind of folks we're accustomed to seeing in church. For example, the second wedding I officiated there was between a prostitute and her former pimp. That ought to give you a pretty good idea for the kind of "clientele" we were dealing with.

But there was little doubt in our minds that God had called Donna and me to Buffalo. To this place. To these people. I could have applied for work at ten thousand empty churches around the country, hoping to find a comfortable place to minister. Instead we moved into the "hood," considering it prime real estate for kingdom expansion.

And though it was certainly a challenge, it was never dull. Nearly every day provided me something new and untried to experience. We shared Christ and tried our best to demonstrate his love. Our church didn't just *serve* the poor; we *were* the poor—a motley blend of the homeless and struggling.

A few brave believers from outside occasionally ventured into our urban center of town, distributing what I called "clothes and cheese" to the underprivileged. I was probably a little too harsh at the time in my feelings and comments about their benevolent efforts. I mean, at least they were *coming* while most others were pretending we didn't even exist. But I knew if the church was going to make a real difference inside this depressing maze of the inner city, we couldn't just tell the people who lived there what Jesus was like and what he could do for them. We couldn't just magically appear on Saturday mornings and then evaporate back into our weekends before the rest of the day got away from us. We couldn't just bait them with handouts and hand-me-downs. We needed to *show* them how this kingdom worked if we expected the people in our neighborhood to get it.

So work we did.

Among other things we started a job creation initiative. People in our church would come up with a small business of some kind and then employ one another to staff it. Some might argue that we were involving the church in areas outside its jurisdiction by putting ministry and money-making concerns within too close proximity to one another. But I doubt any critics of our plan had ever lived among the generationally poor in the inner city. All I know is that we saw some of the hopelessly impoverished among us developing a solid work ethic for the first time in their lives. Some of the unemployed in our church discovered a fresh desire to "provide" for their own families (1 Tim. 5:8). Some on the outside who previously hadn't wanted anything to do with Jesus or his hypocritical followers were not only changing their tunes but also changing their kingdoms as Christ brought redemption to their hungry hearts.

No, we were not a big church and certainly not influential by any stretch. Nothing about us would have caused people to notice we were even there—not until our little church started becoming more than just a meeting space. Not until we became the spitting image of what the kingdom of God is supposed to look like on earth: a bunch of otherwise incompatible people changed by the power of the gospel, sent out to rescue the lost and broken, and living our new lives in shared community with one another for the glory of God.

They noticed us *then*.

The same way they'll notice you.

Turns out that no church sign can attract the world's attention like a church whose life is a sign of the kingdom.

Window Shopping

In the last chapter we began constructing a subversive plan of action for ourselves and the church by defining our mission in terms of *God's* mission—the establishment of his glory on earth. We saw that nothing accomplishes this goal like the redemption of sinners from the bondage of this worldly domain into the light of God's eternal kingdom and that we as his church are the messengers of his salvation to the ends of the earth.

That's some big-time, worldwide subversion going on.

But lest we view this practice as being very one-dimensional, lest we consider our agent duties to be mere appointments on the calendar, contained to certain days of the week, we do well to remember that the church is a 24/7 representation of who God is and what he has done in us. Subversive living is not as simple (or as hard) as making a gospel presentation. As much as God accomplishes through our outward-focused efforts and ministries, he can do amazing things just through the visible interactivity of God's people living our sold-out lives together, day in and day out for our King and his kingdom.

In this sense the church is a present-day *sign* of the kingdom of God.

We are signs of the kingdom in our confession and repentance, demonstrating our need for Christ, showing that God's acceptance of us is based not on what we do for him but on what our Lord Jesus has done on our behalf (and theirs).

We are signs of the kingdom in our humility as we live together in dependence upon him for our daily needs, as we defer to one another instead of seeking to be recognized or to make a name for ourselves, as we welcome outsiders into our midst as full partners and partakers of the gospel.

We are signs of the kingdom when we show and tell others that Christ is sufficient for us during the varied and invariable sufferings of life, that his kingdom is a place where difficult circumstances may intrude but can never rule—not for those who are already at home in an eternal, never-ending relationship with him.

We are signs of the kingdom as seen in the overall Godward trajectory of our lives, despite the fact that in certain singular moments we are far less faithful and godly than we mean to be. So, no, we aren't perfect, as both we and the world would wholeheartedly agree. But our *King* is perfect, and his kingdom keeps drawing out the best in us.

In living together as God's people under his reign and lordship, our churches provide to the world the closest resemblance of the kingdom of God on this side of eternity. We are the invisible kingdom made visible through the people of God and their shared lives on earth.

We are the church.

Where the world comes to window shop.

To see if they're "buying it."

I recently traveled on business to New York City to teach at Gordon-Conwell Seminary and preach at a local church. As I often do, I seized the opportunity to take one of my daughters with me. It was her first time there, so as part of the trip, we planned to take a swing through Manhattan and let her see the sights. We were able to visit the American Girl store. We also went to a Broadway show among other fun things. But as you can attest if you've ever been there, you don't need to be going anywhere in particular to be captivated by the aura of what's happening around you. New York City feeds a person's attention deficit disorder. As someone who could probably benefit greatly from Ritalin if I ever decided to take it, New York City overload is almost too much. Everywhere we turned, we found ourselves in front of another store or shop, drawn to those huge window displays, each one enticing us to come inside and see what else was back there—to find out how it looked up close, how it felt in your hand, what it was really like behind the glass.

The window made you want it.

Our churches are meant to serve the same sort of function. We are God's "store window" on earth where he shows off his kingdom. German author Wolfgang Simson carried the idea even further when he said:

> Jesus has given us the commission to go and make disciples of all nations. It is the growing conviction of many Christians around the world that this will only be achieved by having a church—God's shop window—within walking distance of every person on the globe.[1]

By seeing us, they should see God's kingdom at work.

The world, as we know from both the Bible and personal experience, is passing away, while at the same time Christ is building up his kingdom through the church. He is creating an "already" brand of people who (individually, yes, but especially when seen collectively as a whole) are able to preview the "not yets" of his eternal rule and reign. What others may not be able to grasp spiritually or intellectually about his gospel and his kingdom, they should be able to see physically through the way Christ's people operate together and through the lives that are transformed from their subversive work.

When the outside world peers into your church window and sees you displaying a genuine sense of unity and peace in your relationships, sees you redemptively handling conflict, sees you actively serving your community, sees you living with high levels of integrity and grace, they form an impression. When one of your outreaches is written up favorably in the newspaper, or touches someone in their family, or makes them question what they've always thought about God and the church, they make note of it. They recognize a difference between their experience and yours—between the kingdom of this world and the kingdom of God. And that leaves them with a decision for how they're going to respond.

Now granted, we're not in a popularity contest, and the Bible certainly makes clear that the church will never escape being maligned and misunderstood on earth. Getting others' acceptance of us is not the goal of our kingdom efforts, nor is it how we determine the success of our job performance. Our team at LifeWay Research recently polled a sampling of unchurched twenty-somethings—young men and women who, other than for a wedding, holiday, or funeral, hadn't set foot inside a house of worship of any kind for six months or more—and asked them to agree or disagree with certain statements. When offered the chance to give their opinion on whether or not "Christians get on my nerves," a full 44 percent said this described their feelings pretty well.

OK, duly noted. And no big surprise. But while the world will always hate certain things about faithfully practiced

Christianity, while the cross will always be a stumbling block in many people's minds, while some will always find our views and beliefs to be morally distasteful to their liking, they should at least be able to recognize by looking at us that belonging to Jesus makes people different.

We love one another.

We care about the hurting.

We forgive unfairness.

We live with uncommon character.

We actively serve.

We worship our King.

We share our time.

We give our all.

No, this doesn't mean we awaken every morning without difficulties, problems, and struggles. We've been known to argue with our spouses. We are often in the wrong. We're not always the parents we should be. We're tempted to ignore our neighbors rather than love them.

But by his grace we are followers of Jesus Christ, living out an authentic faith every day of the week, being shaped and sanctified morning by morning through the living Word of God. We're making wholesome and healthy choices with our lifestyles. We're relating to one another with both under-standing kindness and challenging exhortation. We're getting real with one another about what truly matters instead of just floating along and pretending everything is probably all right.

We are signs of the kingdom, windows to the world.

"So look inside," we're saying. "Check us out—broken

people put together through the redeeming power of Christ. None of this is artificially touched up or falsely advertised. This is what life is really like when you're not just out there like everybody else, trailing along behind the latest thing or marching in lockstep with the world's predictable, pop-star mentalities. This is how it feels to be actively and excitedly engaged in transforming the culture instead of just being marketed by it and pigeonholed within it.

"Come back here behind the counter where we keep the keys of the kingdom, and see what happens when you're set free from your bondage to sin and addiction, to your own litany of unnamed dreads and others' fickle opinions. Imagine getting to live every day in a place like this, surrounded by people who take your concerns to heart, who will go to the mat for you, who will be praying for you when you don't even know about it, who will invite and involve you on subversive missions that'll make you wonder why you once thought hanging out at the bar or going clothes shopping was the most fulfilling way to spend a weekend."

We're not just "doing church" here. Every week when we meet to worship, every time we serve our King together in public places, every time we interact with one another on the job or around the lunch table, every time we serve one another and serve our neighbors, we're polishing up the store window. We're letting people get a clearer look inside, to see what this King and his kingdom are all about.

Now if they don't like what they see and aren't interested in coming any closer, they certainly wouldn't be the first to reject the church as being irrelevant and unnecessary. But at least don't let it be because we didn't present our Lord well or didn't realize that others were paying attention.

Yes, they are. And yes, we must.

Window Treatments

Truth is, thinking about the church as a sign of the kingdom goes against much of our religious culture. As mentioned in the previous chapter, we can sometimes put our focus on catering to people who only see the church as a place to receive religious goods and services. They come to see if the music is nice, if their kids will have fun, if the preacher makes them think but also knows how to make them laugh. If everything suits them and wraps up in time so they can beat the crowd to the restaurant for lunch, they feel satisfied they've gotten what they paid for. If not, they'll go looking around somewhere else for better music, better preaching, better programs for the kids . . . a better all-around feeling.

And yet a church that spends most of its time cleaning the windows just so people will come and hopefully stay will only end up obscuring others' view of God's kingdom. When a church allows itself to become little more than a destination point, cluttering it up with lots of props and decorations, their window actually blocks people's view of the glory of God rather than vividly displaying it. People may come and see a show, but they won't see all that God is really doing (and is *able* to do) among those who call him King. They'll only get a small part of the much bigger and much better picture.

Churches are not peddlers of Christian goods and services;

we are cells of subversion and transformation. We're not just opening our doors and hoping for a good turnout; we're opening our lives to show off the glory of our Savior by the way we live together, by the way we serve together, by the way we reach out in Jesus' name together.

To the extent that we keep the focus here—where it needs to be—our window stays clean and our impact significant. We perform the role we were intended to play. We shine like a lighthouse on a stormy night, beaming lifesaving shafts onto the rocky coastline below, where everybody can see it and follow it and be led to real safety. But if we keep ourselves huddled inside, more concerned with making budget than making a difference, we will reduce what others see of our King and his kingdom through us. Nice but not exactly noteworthy. Hinted at but not held out there with both hands so people can see what this is all about—and *who* it's all about—by the way we interact with one another and interface with the culture. Unless we're serious about displaying the difference God makes in us and wants to make in them, they won't be captivated by the joys of daily kingdom living and the visible power of our King.

They'll miss the sign if it's not lit up.

When my daughter and I came out of that Broadway play on our trip back East, we emerged from the theater into nightfall on New York City. From there we took the subway back to our hotel, located not far from Times Square. Yes, we had seen that area during the daytime when we'd left several hours before. That was one way of looking at it. But to come up out of that subway station after dark, to see the city ablaze with light and glow and activity . . . my little girl just popped her hand to her mouth and slowly began spinning around and around, trying to take in the spectacle. Amazing.

That's how bright our light should be.

That's how bright our light *can* be.

Not just church—*changed lives!*

The subversive kingdom has come near, and the church has sprung up to carry out this kingdom mission. Jesus, "the true light, who gives light to everyone," has come to this planet (John 1:9) and has deposited little groupings of disciples on earth to be the "light of the world" (Matt. 5:14)—*his church!* But we don't do it by constructing fancier buildings or outdoing the programs offered by other congregations. We do it by just faithfully living out our callings together as representatives of God's kingdom. We do it—as Paul said, for example—by even the little things like dealing with internal differences "without grumbling and arguing" (Phil. 2:14).

By living out the Word in real life and real time, we engage the King's mission on a subversive level. We no longer come across as paid salesmen for God trying to build our own self-esteem and bank account by closing a deal (memorized presentation and all). Kingdom citizens come across as satisfied customers embracing all of life with the King. We are living with the benefits that should include better marriages, relationships, and overall approaches to life.

Kingdom citizens subvert by ascribing value to people who on the surface wouldn't seem to appeal to us. By sharing freely and generously so our brothers and sisters in Christ are cared for and ministered to shows the same kind of sacrificial compassion for all the others God leads us to serve, both in our community and around the globe.

This is what makes us "shine like stars in the world," showing ourselves changed by Christ Jesus into people who are "blameless and pure, children of God who are faultless in a crooked and perverted generation" (v. 15). Such offhand but on-purpose opportunities are how we represent something bigger and more eternal than ourselves to those around us. It's how God uses us to reveal his nature, character, and mercy powerfully enough to others that they fall on their faces and worship him, saying, "God is truly among you" (1 Cor. 14:25).

Then our light keeps pushing back the darkness and drawing people to the flame.

Aliens and Ambassadors

I've said this before, but it bears repeating because the whole world system is working at convincing us this isn't true. One of the reasons we don't do a better job of keeping the lights cranked up in our window is because we forget how dark the world outside really is. We interpret the cultural situation around us as being more late afternoon than the dead of midnight. And since most everybody seems to be having such a good time out there, enjoying their pizza and fantasy football, we end up being more motivated just to compete for their Sunday attention than to represent before them the Christ-transformed life they so desperately, desperately need.

So we pull the blinds most weeknights and see what's on television. We pour ourselves into our work and avoid the homeless man on the sidewalk as we're walking to our car. We don't like to think or be reminded how bad the conditions are around us, how deeply people are suffering, how many ways our lack of kingdom presence steals hope from those who need the Lord whether they know it or not.

I mean, we've got our own problems. We're working hard to save for stuff and lower our debt exposure. We're busy with the things happening in the lives of those close to us. We don't really have time to be more active with our fellow church members than we already are because we're so heavily invested everywhere else. In fact, just thinking about getting more involved as a church in tangling with the chronic ills of the world around us adds a layer of complication to our lives we don't see how we can really afford.

Can't we just keep doing church the way we've always done it? People seemed fairly happy with that.

But not when we realize God has stationed us here as an outpost of light because the world is so broken. Not when we realize that we're in rebellion against the world's rebellion. Not when we realize the vast difference between a life transformed by Christ and a life that's attempted any other way. We are not just a light in the darkness; we are light in the *deepest* darkness. With the needs as great as they are and the stakes at such a high level, the church cannot just be a candle in the wind; it needs to be a city of blinding lights (with apologies to both Elton John and U2).

So get out there and look. See what's really happening. Spend some time with people who are hurting and fatigued and hungry and lonely, and you'll understand why they need a place where the lights are on and the kingdom is shining brightly.

Subversives simply aren't fooled by a world masquerading as cool and normal. Nor have they lost their confidence in the gospel and its transforming qualities, in its incomparable ability to change people's lives. They see clearly enough to recognize just how dark the times are, and they totally grasp the pressing, critical nature of the church's role in countering a world system that's lost in sin and suffering the sure consequences.

This is serious. And it's time we all started thinking that way.

Not same-old, same-old. *Subversive.*

The Bible gives us two ways for the church to view ourselves amid the harsh climate of our hostile culture: as both *aliens* and *ambassadors.* Peter wrote to the churches of his day:

> I urge you as aliens and temporary residents to abstain from fleshly desires that war against you. Conduct yourselves honorably among the Gentiles, so that in a case where they speak against you as those who do evil, they may, by observing your good works, glorify God in a day of visitation. (1 Pet. 2:11–12)

My kids love to tell people that I married an alien since my wife is originally from Canada and was a Canadian citizen when we married. They sometimes tell their friends, "Did you know our mom is an alien?" (You can imagine how much she loves that.) But truly we kingdom citizens are "aliens and temporary residents" on this earth, sent to carry out an insurrection of light against the world's rebellion. And if we have any hope of doing our part well, we cannot cave to the temptation of blending into the fabric of this world or deciding we half-prefer its way of living over ours.

People don't need to see any more status-quo examples, especially from the church. There are more than enough of those to go around. What the world needs to see are people who stay true to the values of another kingdom, who stand apart by aligning themselves with another King. And to do so, we need to remind ourselves constantly that our citizenship actually resides elsewhere.

We're aliens. Get used to it.

But we're not just here to stand around and be different. We have been given these kingdom distinctions so we can serve in the role of "ambassadors" (2 Cor. 5:20). We are "sent people," meeting other people in their home countries, building relationships at close range from the "embassy" we know as the Christian church—God's kingdom outpost on earth.

We do possess one key difference, however, from the type of ambassadors that would have been most familiar to Paul's audience in the New Testament era. During the days of the Roman Empire, ambassadors were more likely to be diplomatic officials of lesser nations, dispatched for the purpose of negotiating peaceful terms with the Roman juggernaut. Rome, on the other hand, sent out armies, followed by governors, to rule those they had conquered. The strong did not send out ambassadors in those days; the weak did.

But as ambassadors of God's subversive kingdom, the church does just the opposite. We are positioned on earth to represent the King of the entire universe, sent into the weaker, more unstable confines of the broken world, on mission to rescue those who are rebelling against Christ's rule and reign. Rather then sitting back hoping the world finds *us,* we go out into the world under the authority of Almighty God himself, seeking to establish relationship with those who are far away from him, those in bondage to a culture that is darker than they know.

We're ambassadors. Get into it.

Keller, Texas, is a wealthy, mostly white suburb north of Fort Worth, yet it is also home to citizens and immigrants from many countries of the world: Indians, Koreans, Chinese, Malaysians, Mexicans, Laotians, Iranians, Vietnamese, and a full range of others. As natives of distant nations, these trans-plants—even if Christian—are not immediately at home in the normal life and dynamic of an American church. Add to that the significant percentage who are resistant to Christian faith to begin with, and the field for subversive action is wide for kingdom agents, aliens, and ambassadors.

Into this melting pot of possibilities, NorthWood Church and its Global Impact ministry is attempting to bridge the gap between themselves and these various people groups. One simple way they're accomplishing this goal is by hosting fellow-ship meals. NorthWood seeks to establish relationships with these men, women, and families of other lands around a com-mon table, sharing both their food and their hearts with them. They took heat several years ago for inviting about a thousand Muslim citizens from the greater Dallas-Fort Worth area, just to come engage with them and get acquainted. Then more than twenty-five hundred showed up—proving the church's point that respect and friendship is key to establishing opportunities for Muslims to hear of our faith in Jesus Christ.

Churches that don't embrace their role as kingdom ambassadors would find ignoring these representatives of other cultures easier than reaching out to them. Churches like NorthWood, however, see it differently. Every time I've spoken there, I meet someone from somewhere else with a remarkable story of life change. NorthWood Church and their pastor, Bob Roberts, see an opportunity for their church to put its window on wide display, to shine kingdom light in places where more people than ever can be intrigued by it, warmed by it, and ultimately transformed by it.

God's purpose in sending Christ, and then sending the church, is so a world in rebellion can see his desire to establish relationship with them. And we are now his ambassadors, representatives of Christ himself, demonstrating how people can experience life in his kingdom. We do it by going, we do it by proclaiming his truth with clarity, but we also do it just by walking "wisely toward outsiders," responding to one another with speech that is always "gracious," with lives that are "seasoned with salt" (Col. 4:4–5), with Christian relationships that illuminate the gospel without saying a word in a dark—oh, how miserably dark, dark world.

Good Sign

I collect funny signs. Pictures of them, anyway. And when I speak at conferences, I often put a few of them up on the screen where people can see them and laugh at them. Every Friday on my blog (www.edstetzer.com) I share my "church signs of the week"—and there are lots of funny ones (often for the very reason churches don't intend to be funny).

But it's easy to get signs confused. I've got a "Keep Right" sign that I snapped at an airport. The arrow underneath it points left.

I've got a British sign that reads, "For Three Pounds, We Will Shoot Your Kid." I'm hoping it has something to do with photography.

Then there's always the "Kids with Gas Eat Free" sign—the gold standard of badly whacked roadside syntax.

I never cease to be amazed at directional signs and advertisements like these that go up with so little forethought as to how they're worded or what they might be communicating to others. And yet I wonder if we do the same thing in our churches—just going along, tacking up our announcements and activities, too busy to check and see if we're saying what we mean to say. We get together and do our church things. We think we're sprucing up our image. But are we truly pointing people toward the kingdom? Are we a good sign of what life with God is supposed to be like?

A church that doesn't point others to the kingdom is a bad sign. Or, like many bad signs, a church can even become cause for laughter and scorn among outsiders. Either way, this is not what God expects from us.

Too many of our churches are pointing the wrong direction. And I'm not just talking about the "church" as an institution; I'm talking about the people who make it up and are called to display God's kingdom realities from within it. *I'm talking about us!* Some of us are bad signs because we're not in unity with one another. Some of us are bad signs because we've abandoned our confidence in the gospel or have accepted false doctrine into our teaching. Others of us may not have lost sight of gospel truth, but we look more like a social club than dedicated insurgents engaged in picking off captives from the kingdom of darkness.

What does *your* church sign say?

And how are you helping to say it better?

Maybe we should all consider taking our signs down and going underground to get our lives together to match our proclamation. Then we can put out a proud "Grand Reopening: Under New Management." It's time our churches started reflecting a clear, noticeable, unmistakable kingdom difference. It's time we became known as a place where husbands and wives remain lovingly committed to each other and where marriages that have stopped operating well are restored to thrive once again. It's time we became known as a place where families are strengthened and children are raised to be lovers of God and defenders of their faith. It's time we became known as a place where orphans are cared for, where the lonely and widows are embraced in community, where races are reconciled, and where the hurting find genuine help at the loving, caring, redemptive hand of God's people.

The world "window-shops" the gospel as they observe our way of living. They make their determinations by the kind of signs we accurately display. Strangely enough, then, one of our most effective ways of being subversive is to make our kingdom lives too obvious to ignore.

We are the city on the hill.

We are Times Square in the darkness.

We are the church of the living God.

Now live like it.

10

Instrumentality

I've noticed a strange phenomenon in some churches: we like to hear people tell us the hard things we know we should be doing. We somehow seem to like it when the preacher goes all Dr. Phil on us, busting us flatfooted in our complacency and worldliness. Sitting there in Sunday-morning mode, cocooned for a moment from our usual weekday feelings, many of us respond with hearty amens and applause to these passioned appeals for deeper Christian conviction. We feel it. We get it. We want it.

But that doesn't mean we're actually going to do it.

Yes, pondering what it's like to be spiritually surrendered makes us want to get out our notebooks and start making lists, schedules, and outlines. We're drawn to the idea of deep-down, godly dedication and commitment. We genu-inely admire those folks, for example, who pursue a life of countercultural simplicity, who've seen through the fatigue factor that's involved in the nonstop self-promotion of our personal "brands" and are able to be more singularly focused on Christ. We're inspired by those who build quiet track records of unwavering faithfulness over ten, twenty, thirty, forty years or more. In fact, we may catch ourselves one Tuesday morning still thinking about something we heard a missionary family report during Sunday's service that week. We're captivated by the life-changing reach of their daily work.

But that doesn't mean we'll actually become any more courageous, consistent, or useful ourselves. We're still more likely to follow the world's *zig* instead of the kingdom's *zag*.

And you know what? That's just not very subversive.

So let's be big enough to admit that in far too many ways we and our churches have been like the compliant son in Jesus' parable, the one who told his father, "Sure, Dad, I'd be happy to go work in your vineyard today, just like you asked." He gave every indication of obedience and said all the things that were expected of him. But when it came right down to it, well . . .

"He didn't go" (Matt. 21:30). He may well have meant to do it, may have always wanted to be the kind of son his father could count on to do what he said. But he wasn't. When push came to shove, he shoved off in the other direction.

The more we get in touch with the nature of God's subversive kingdom, the more we realize he wants to use us in his mission of seeking and saving the lost from the dark captivity of this world. He wants our lives and our churches to be picture windows displaying his glory, to be trophy cases that highlight what his redemption can do in receptive human hearts. Basically, he just wants us to be *instruments* in his hand—each one of us differently sized and shaped, of course, each one serving the unique assignments he's given us, but each one radically obedient, each one primed for action, each one eager to be turned loose wherever he calls us to go.

Is that descriptive of us?

Is that descriptive of our churches? Of you and *your* church?

Granted, like the *other* son in Jesus' parable, we may drag behind us a long history of telling our Father, "I don't want to" (v. 29) when he directs us to go into various "vineyards" of kingdom service. Your church and mine may have been long resistant to putting ourselves out there where God could do some of his best subverting work through us. We may have shied away from the pressure of feeling constantly on call when it comes to kingdom opportunities. But let's decide right now that we're going to adjust the way this scene has typically played out in our lives. Let's change our minds and go.

Let's consider ourselves willing, ready, and available.

Even instrumental.

Integrated Instrumentation

The church is the instrument God uses to lead others into his kingdom through our proclamation and demonstration of his saving, transforming gospel. This is why we say the church is gathered to be scattered. We're exhorted to be exported. The church is not intended just to give us regular, weekly reminders of biblical truth—tough talk that we may or may not take to heart or consistently take with us into real life. In order for this kingdom plan to be effective, we need to let all this hard teaching we hear not just go into one ear but go out through both feet.

Yet it's actually even more than that. Because of the supreme position God has ordained for the church in carrying out this all-consuming role, the only way to turn this fresh resolve into a truly powerful, subversive plan of action is for us to unite together as one body to do it.

So on the off chance that you've gotten this far in the book and still think the best way to be a real agent of change in the world is by doing a work-around of the church, I want to reiterate that the Scripture describes the church as God's primary tool for overthrowing short-lived world rebellion in which we've lived for millennia. Together we are the steady battering ram our God has created to help establish his own kingdom by tearing down the enemy's kingdom, piece by stubborn piece. If your understanding of what it means to be a kingdom "instrument" trends more *individual* than *in tandem* with other believers, the Word makes clear that it behooves us to maintain a kingdom agenda within our local bodies, not to give up on them and try going it alone. The church may not be perfect—by a long shot—but the church is still God's chosen instrument for gospel insurgency.

I believe one of the most compelling descriptions of this design occurs when Paul ties the glorious mission of Jesus to the mission of the church by declaring that God has put "everything" under Christ's feet, "and appointed Him as head over everything *for the church,* which is His body, the fullness of the One who fills all things in every way" (Eph. 1:22–23, italics added).

The idea that God has instigated an act this powerful and magnificent—specifically "for the church"—is just fascinating to me. Paul's language speaks to the special, unique role God has chosen for us in his revolutionary mission to reclaim the world. The church is not merely a voluntary organization that gets together for weekly meetings. It's not some place we come just to get our needs met and our spirits fed, as if happening in a parallel universe apart from his larger program of rescuing captives from the broken world. God the Father has done something completely game-changing both for and through his Son, putting "everything under His feet." And he has done it so the church can have the right and the ability to join him on his glorious mission.

This is huge. We're not just *like* a body—a mere analogy that works since our various parts do fit together to form a cohesive whole. We actually *are* a body—"His body"—the body of Jesus Christ. We have a purpose that's much greater than our individual purposes alone, and we find this purpose by teaming up with one another in shared kingdom adventure.

But that's not all. As the apostle Paul continues to unpack this grand, master plan of the ages, we notice that God inspired him to describe the church as "the fullness of the One who fills all things in every way"—a phrase that sounds so biblically obvious, we're tempted to skim over it and trust we probably get the gist of it. But think about this phrase a little harder than usual. What is Paul saying? I'll admit, it does almost read like some of my late night e-mails, but there's actually real power in this roundabout way of saying things. I think we can summarize it in two points: (1) Jesus directs the fullness of himself toward the life and ministry of the church, and (2) as a result, the church's mission is to fill up and fill out Christ's kingdom mission, to employ his empowering "fullness" to animate our subversive activity.

He brings all of himself *to* us.

And he fulfills his intended mission *through* us.

Together we are instruments of his kingdom.

Notice how many plural personal pronouns the Lord stuck into the following statement from this same chapter of Ephesians—a long, winding sentence that's so busy covering theological ground, Paul couldn't seem to bring himself to close it off before he got the whole thing off his chest.

> In him we have redemption through his blood, the forgiveness of our trespasses, according to the riches of his grace, which he lavished upon us, in all wisdom and insight making known to us the mystery of his will, according to his purpose, which he set forth in Christ as a plan for the fullness of time, to unite all things in him, things in heaven and things on earth. (Eph. 1:7–10 ESV)

God's goal in history is to bring everything together under the authority of Jesus Christ. And we, his church, his body—his redeemed and divinely resourced band of brothers and sisters—possess both the privilege and the purpose of being called to this mission.

I hope this doesn't only make you hungry to do God's will more fully and faithfully yourself. I hope it makes you want to join together with other believers in the church, perhaps as soon as tomorrow afternoon, itching to follow Christ's purposeful lead in your lives, multiplying the compassion and creativity of your efforts. I hope it helps you recognize the vast scope of what God is up to around here, not only in the church at large but in the church at your street address.

I hope it makes you love your church and see its potential like never before.

I think I've mentioned I lead LifeWay Research, an entity that (we believe) is a leading supplier of smart, timely analysis for Christians who are devoted to accurately perceiving and subverting modern culture. Naturally we conduct a lot of studies and report a lot of statistics. And sometimes the numbers don't portray the church in too favorable of a light.

Interestingly we've found two extreme opinions at work around this subject. The opinions are similar to two little brothers on a playground. The older brother can torture his little brother all he wants. But *you* can't—or else you are in big trouble. The same is true with the church. *First,* many people (even Christians) maintain a negative view of the church. *Second,* Christians have a defensive reaction toward anything uncomplimentary that's said or concluded about the church. So telling the truth about the church is controversial at best. People tend to get upset when others are critical of it—or when they're not critical enough.

Hmm. What do we do with that?

Number one, I believe we must stay *honest but honoring* in our valuing of the church. We cannot love Jesus and despise his bride because the church will always be essential to his subversive mission on earth. And though we stay objective in our critique, not blindly glossing over its flaws or overlooking those matters that weaken its message and purity, biblical truth calls us to keep a high view of the church and of our instrumental role within it.

Number two, we must ascribe to the church *reason for hope,* knowing that Jesus himself has promised great things for it—namely that "the forces of Hades will not overpower it" (Matt. 16:18). Neither the truth about how the church is performing its role today nor the way it is currently perceived among people both inside and outside can threaten what Christ will ultimately accomplish through it. The church is his instrument, even when it's fussy and fidgety in his hand.

Yes, love the Lord.

And yes, love his church.

And learn to love doing what he desires to do through us.

Disciple Making

Chief among the building blocks of our subversive plan of action is our exaltation of God's glory on earth. We talked about that a few chapters back. And the more people who are drawn into faith-based, grace-filled relationship with him through belief in his marvelous gospel, the more his glory explodes in the darkened, depressing corners of our cities and towns, of our nation and our world. His glory and his gospel form the cornerstones of our missional attack.

Also important, besides the pervasive spreading of the gospel, is the daily, living testimony we exhibit to the world through the church. Our conduct toward one another, teamed with our sacrificial compassion toward the overlooked and undervalued, paints a tangible portrait of our King and the desirable realities of his rule. The lives we lead are a visible sign of the kingdom, one that lights up the night around us.

But intertwined in here is another important leg of our action plan—the process of *making disciples*—a priority of the church as God continues to expand his kingdom in the world.

Following his resurrection and near the end of his earthly ministry, Jesus announced to his disciples the mandate we now know as the Great Commission, a statement loaded with implications for the subversive kingdom.

Go, therefore, and make disciples of all nations, baptizing them in the name of the Father and of the Son and of the Holy Spirit, teaching them to observe everything I have commanded you. And remember, I am with you always, to the end of the age. (Matt. 28:19–20)

Go.
Make disciples.
Baptize. Teach. Inspire.
Truly, nothing melts away the bitter cold of a broken world faster than the exponential heat of one person discipling another, two discipling two, four discipling four, until new,

mature believers are springing up and spreading like wildfire throughout the enemy camp—sincere, subversive makers of even more disciple makers.

This development of spiritual growth and grounding among God's people, especially when applied to the eager hearts of new Christians, populates the church with biblically trained insurgents whose love for seeing God's lost children found is only rivaled by seeing his found children fed. The kingdom grows at its most healthy pace when churches are taking seriously the task of rooting people's faith in the full counsel of God.

This wisdom inspired Dawson Trotman to seize the discipleship directive of 2 Timothy 2:2 and begin multiplying his passion for engaging others in prayer, study, teaching, and Scripture memory. Trotman was no preacher, just a lumberyard worker. But challenged in 1933 by Paul's exhortation to take "what you have learned from me in the presence of many witnesses" and commit it to "faithful men who will be able to teach others also," he sparked a movement that today equips people from all walks of life with tools to help them lead others deeper in the faith. Business professionals, trade workers, students, homemakers—millions have been taken deeper in the Word (and become more subversively dangerous in the field) by the expansive reach of the Navigators and their seasoned discipleship groups.

Trotman didn't set out to build an organization. He started with high school students, then with Sunday school classes, then with sailors aboard the USS *West Virginia* during World War II. And when one person was taught, that person became the teacher of another. And another. And another. More than seventy-five years later, this same one-on-one Navigators strategy is at work among as many as seventy nationalities in more than a hundred countries.

Going and making disciples works.

It seriously subverts.

But the reason why it does is not just because someone came up with a good method. Your church's plan and program for getting young, untested believers entrenched in God's truth—and your role in being a part of it—won't really be what grows the ground troops among you. Like everything else it all starts with Jesus and his glory-producing purpose . . . and with some words that go along with his Great Commission but are not often treated to the same fanfare and hallway banners as the "go" and "make disciples" part.

Verse 18—immediately prior, and yet routinely skipped over, seemingly out of place and disjointed from the rest: "All authority has been given to Me in heaven and on earth."

"All authority."

Those words should mean a lot to us as we've talked about rule and reign. God has always ruled sovereignly over the universe. When Jesus arrived, he declared that the kingdom had come near. Then right before giving the Great Commission, he told them, "All authority is mine." King Jesus was reminding them about his rule, telling them to tell the world about him so they might submit to that rule.

Christ has declared the truth of his sovereign intentions while also revealing the raw power behind whatever breakthroughs we make into the kingdom of darkness. And it begins and ends with his authority—both his might and his mission to expand the kingdom at his will, through his disciples, in your church. Everywhere his people are diligent in their disciple making, subversion is sure to kick into high gear. By reversing the effects of the fall, by anchoring Christian faith in biblical concrete, the ultimate collapse of the power of the rebellious world feels that much closer.

And that's as it should be.

But let me tell you what can sometimes be more feel good than freedom ringing, and I saw it firsthand at a conference in Manhattan a couple of years ago. I was speaking on the kingdom of God to a responsive group of evangelical Presbyterians, Baptists, and nondenominational Christians in a building that had once been the seemingly thriving home to a mainline church for many years. This now-defunct mainline congregation had wanted to be engaged in the kingdom. They thought they were making a God-sized dent in the problems of people around them. But they were mistakenly convinced that the kingdom of God could be ushered in through mere relief and aid activities, through an effort to manufacture a better society. Embracing a theology widely categorized as the "social gospel," they elevated their pursuit of human justice above the eternal priority of the gospel and Great Commission. And by getting distracted from the true mission of the church, their theology became unrecognizable from former days and their candlestick burned out before their eyes. Their building was now a meeting hall we rented to talk about engaging in God's kingdom mission.

Listen, devoted followers of Christ and his subversive

kingdom will do a lot of caring, compassionate work. They'll alleviate the plight of the poor, doctor the sick, and stand up against social and racial injustices of all kinds—no matter how many or how often some well-meaning believers tell them *justice* is a bad word, that it's an uncomfortable stance for churches to take and actively participate in. But having said that, the kingdom of God will not arise from the social advances of efforts such as these. Jesus will finalize his kingdom whenever he deems the time eternally appropriate, and our chief job in this hour as instruments of his grace is to see that people are saved and disciples are made. Because when biblically articulate disciples go out to do the revolutionary work of their King, they'll transform their communities as God works through them to build new disciples from the ground up.

Changed Communities

No, we're not going to make our world *all* better. Hate to break it to you. That's United Nations talk. That's Olympic opening ceremonies talk. That's activist groups bullhorning in the streets talk. But it's not Bible talk, nor is it reality.

Yes, by the common mercies of God, he will use us to address certain issues for the liberation of our communities. And as long as we're not expecting to see every ill eradicated on our way to a heaven-on-earth experience, we are free to be turned loose by God on mercy missions that strike hard at human need while also infusing our outreaches with the gospel and follow-up discipleship.

Some churches and their concerned members focus hard on poverty, others on stopping sex trafficking, others on adopting and caring for orphans and abandoned children. You name it; we do it. And when we enter these situations at the behest of God's Spirit, our ministry hearts can resonate openly with the love and compassion of Christ.

Mark Swanson is doing this very thing through Mission Vancouver, a ministry of Grace Vancouver Church, attempting to reach a city considered by even some secular observers to be (as Mark's online site says), a place "where an entire generation has been raised without God."

> It is a city of breathtaking beauty, a truly international city, filled with culture and diversity. It is also a city of great loneliness, spiritual apathy, and secularism on a scale unlike any other city in North America.[1]

Mark, a longtime lay leader and now associate pastor at Grace Vancouver, sees this transformational focus as being vital to the church's heartbeat. "Grace formerly had individuals involved in ministry and involving people in ministry," he said in a phone interview. "We are now *requiring* our small groups to adopt a ministry; I consider it a part of discipleship. When we pray for social justice, for outreach, we include the kingdom in the same breath as being what the gospel is about." The deeper purpose behind his many efforts at bringing about change and building relationships, he says, "is to extend the kingdom of God, preaching Christ and making his love known."

So like Mark, with nothing to lose, knowing that "all

authority" is already firmly ensconced in Christ's eternal, resurrected being, we can go about the business of transforming our communities, our country, and yes, even the nations, in every way his Spirit directs us to go.

Just being instruments.

And to God be all glory.

For several months during the life of our church plant in Erie, Pennsylvania, we began the process of constructing an addition to our primary building as well as a new parsonage. Looking to save costs and also to give others the opportunity to share the joys of generosity—(how's that for a holy rationale?)—we invited several volunteer missions teams to come help us, receiving them in grateful waves as the process unfolded. The bricklayers showed up one week, the framers came next, the plumbers next, and the electricians after that. Teams stuffed insulation and hung drywall. They painted. They spilled things. It was a great and crazy time.

I remember in particular one of the framing groups trying to perform their job all week around heavy downpours, which slowed their work and kept them from being able to complete everything they'd come to do. By the time they finally needed to leave, the framed walls were finished but still lying on the ground, unraised. Instead of seeing the skeleton of a new building rising into the air as they drove off, they left instead with nothing but a poured foundation and floor joists to show for all their efforts. It turned out to be the *next* group actually, thanks to a nice turn in the weather, who got to erect the walls, put the roof on, and hang the windows—to experience the visible results of real progress.

That's just the way it is a lot of times—not only with outdoor building projects but also with the complicated labors involved in transforming communities for Christ. Every group that showed up to help us was doing their work as unto the Lord, toiling as hard as they could for the kingdom. But only the people who arrived at the end were able to witness the finished product. Many people serve the kingdom of God through their churches, doing noble work in their cities and neighborhoods. And some of them are privileged to see major changes occur as a result. Others, however, invest just as much energy and try equally hard, only to watch so many things go undone, to experience so many needs that overtax their ability to meet them, and to face so much opposition that thwarts their best planning and their most careful expectations.

But even when you're not the one to see the harvest of real improvement with your own eyes, you can still know you're playing a pivotal part in the healing and restoration of those lives around you, every time you put on your nail apron, your stethoscope, or your walking shoes for Jesus. And you can be *absolutely* sure that your King is working wisely and skillfully to make all things right in the end, just the way he desires them to be.

So our work is not futile when we pursue the hard things God asks us to do, when we yield ourselves to becoming available instruments in his hand. As agents of his subversive kingdom, we don't expect the darkness just to meekly melt away. Every time we push forward, we're not surprised to be on the receiving end of pushback. But our orders are to keep forging ahead into the darkness, making disciples as we go, collecting freed captives along the way, and changing lives for the sake of the gospel and the revelation of God's glory.

If we do that, we're being faithful and responsive.

We're following through on what the Father has told us.

We're not hearing God's thing and then doing our own.

We're proving our kingdom mettle.

We're being instrumental.

Subversive Planning

These subversive plans of attack—the sharing of Christ's gospel near and far, the diligent display of kingdom community, the making of active disciple makers, and the God-glorifying transformation of our neighborhoods as well as the nations—are each worth our time to pursue and our willingness to obey.

This is how subversives team up to do great things.

But our true heart as devoted kingdom agents is to view our efforts as having the true qualities of "salt and light." Just as yeast disappears into the leavened dough, never to be extracted or held up for celebration, *salt* melts into whatever food or substance it's changing, and *light* simply streaks away into the vast reaches of the universe. As salt and light, then, our work is actually the world-changing work of our Lord and King. We join him on his mission. And as long as he receives the credit and honor for it, we know he will derive a full harvest from every bit of labor he inspires through our hands, minds, feet, and shoulders. As Jesus said, "Unless a grain of wheat falls into the ground and dies, it remains by itself. But if it dies, it produces a large crop" (John 12:24).

We're just glad to share the fulfilling adventure.

Fifty years ago Christians were mainstream in America and fully accepted as a cultural norm. We were plenty rebellious in those days, but it was a politically and socially accepted rebellion. We preached loudly and boldly the lostness of man without Christ and his need to have his family in church. We rebelled against atheists and Hugh Hefner. They were not necessarily mad at us, but we were mad at them without apology for the lies and immorality they promoted in our world.

Somewhere over the next fifty years, they got mad back at us and marginalized our faith as being out of touch and culturally unacceptable. As kingdom citizens, we are at a historic crossroads. We can either get mad right back at them again and keep the cycle going (some of us already are, I'm afraid), or we can respond like Jesus. We can adopt subversive agendas as a way of rebelling against the rebellion. And we can become part of the King's mission to rescue those who are far from his kingdom.

Doing the King's work requires us to live *within* the world in some ways and to rebel *against* it in others. God calls us to both. But because we know that he has "already" established himself the victor of his "not yet" experience, we can endure the challenge, suffering, potential rejection, or embarrassment with confident grace and joy. He is sending us on mission to represent his ultimate reign and rule. And just as he will show himself King forever, we treat him as King right now.

He calls. We go. We declare him. We display him.

We are subversive kingdom agents to the end.

Epilogue

The message of the kingdom is subversive at its core, yet this fact is often missed. Perhaps you see it a bit more so after reading this book.

We often hear about the resurrection of Christ but not always about the ongoing rule of Christ—at least not in a way that doesn't overdo end-times predictions and paranoia at the expense of living *right this minute* within the confident glow and aura of his established kingdom victory.

Yet if you hear a message that says Jesus is alive but you don't hear him proclaimed as the reigning King, you're missing a big part of the message. Jesus does rule—better yet, his rule is advancing now! Jesus is Lord. And while this is big news that should brightly color and impact the rest of today—right here in our own season of history—a short look at the past reveals that it was in some ways an even bigger, more obvious deal to people in the first century . . . for more readily accountable reasons.

First-century pagans all agreed on this one statement: "Caesar is Lord." That was the law. Now, in the privacy of one's own home, a person can believe whatever he wants to believe. But when the situation or the civic obligation called for it in Roman times, the blanket custom was to announce "Caesar is Lord"—and to say it like you meant it. It was like the "heil Hitler" of that day. You said it to declare your loyalty to the dictator or emperor. So they could not have picked a more subversive declaration than "Jesus is Lord."

The whole world agreed with this statement, at least for public consumption. And wasn't it obvious? Caesar really *was* lord of the whole known world.

Yet a new kingdom was breaking into the world, and the early Christians (unlike all other people of the era) were known to utter another kind of statement—one that we now sing in worship and wouldn't think anything about wearing around our wrist or on a T-shirt at the fitness center. But to utter some similar yet highly subversive words within a first-century Roman context was . . . well, it wasn't just subversive; it was *treasonous*.

Not "*Caesar* is Lord."

"*Jesus* is Lord."

Yet we seem to have lost much of that subversive impulse today. While the world rebels, too often we've participated in that rebellion—even enjoyed it. Reveling in consumerism, so many Christians have become customers of religious goods and services rather than those who labor together for kingdom work. Too many are customers rather than colaborers.

But when we declare "Jesus is Lord," it changes us. We

rebel against the world's values. We rebel against the dreams of success that don't care about others. We rebel against goals of life that leave out the lost. Why? Because Jesus is Lord.

Those three words changed everything.

And today, though perhaps this statement might cost less in many settings, it should *mean* no less in *any* setting. The world lives with its obvious loyalties to power, religion, greed, sex, and other idols. But *none* of these is our lord. Not anymore. *Jesus* is Lord—a truth that still has the same kind of teeth today as it did when first spoken in first-century clothes. So after all we've seen and experienced about this truth through the pages of this book, how is this supposed to change the way we live? Let me finish with a few simple but significant reminders:

1. *We live in rebellion against the rebellion.* Early on we discussed how God is the rightful Ruler of the universe. He sovereignly rules (and has always ruled) over the entire world. In the Old Testament he ruled from his throne in heaven. But the world, held in bondage to sin, positioned itself in rebellion to the legitimate, right, and good rule of God. All men were held captive to the rule of the enemy.

Yet in Jesus, the kingdom of God came near, breaking into our world and expanding its reach through the new life he gave to men and women as their Redeemer Messiah. Those who received his sinless sacrifice as full payment for their sins became citizens of the kingdom, encouraged and empowered to band together as agents with their fellow brothers and sisters, called to live in rebellion against the rebellion of world kingdom. Jesus becomes Lord, and his people become partakers in his mission to take back what the enemy had stolen.

And yet today the world is still in rebellion. The names and faces have changed but not the status of the world's temporary rebellion—only the fact that his time is shorter, as is our eager wait for the consummated rule of our Lord and Savior, the King of kings. But while we wait, we live in occupied land. We reside on the enemy's ground, even though our hearts belong to another whose ultimate victory, though delayed, is as sure as tomorrow's sunrise.

So this is not a cakewalk here. This is no time to be goofing around. The enemy is on the attack, but we are aware of schemes. The world is broken and lost. The world is in rebellion to God, and we are in rebellion to the world. We are the rebellion against the rebellion.

2. We deconstruct our false view of the kingdom. As we've come to see, God's is a radical and subversive kingdom. Yet this seems a far cry from a safe church filled with religious customers. Many churches today have made the kingdom into the kingdom of religion rather than the kingdom of God. In that world the goal is the survival of the church itself and the comfort of those who line its padded pews. So the end result is, we "grow a great church." But that's not living for a subversive kingdom. Perhaps this is why so many churches are filled with passive spectators rather than active participants in the kingdom mission.

Believers who live as agents of the kingdom are called "colaborers," while most churches seem to be filled with only customers. But if we're going to live out our subversive, rebellious streak in these days of open opposition to the world's system, it can't be normal just to sit and watch when we should be joining in the kingdom mission.

We have been given new life for the King, and we need a different kind of church that takes seriously his rule. Regrettably, we have made it acceptable to sit in church week after week and do nothing and still call ourselves followers of Christ. No longer! King Jesus calls us to more. He calls our churches to stand and subversively fight.

3. *We live as agents and ambassadors of God's kingdom in small, subversive ways.* The kingdom's work is done in small ways by people living as agents of the King.

I work in the research division at one of the largest providers of Christian resources in the country. LifeWay is so big, in fact, that it has its own zip code, with a tunnel running underneath the street that goes to the post office. *It's big.* Yet "bigness" is not our goal. Actually, it may be one of our challenges because the way we make our "biggest" difference is by thinking small, helping pockets and handfuls of Christian groups in churches all over the nation and world seek to live on a kingdom mission.

When I go home from work, I enjoy being part of one of those groups in my own neighborhood. Though I largely spend my day writing, doing research, or traveling to speak, I believe the closest thing I do for kingdom effort is what I do on Sunday night, leading a small group in my neighborhood, ministering and being in community with those who live around me, spending time with five or six families in close, intimate discussion about the things of God.

LifeWay is a support to our kingdom mission, but the kingdom is best displayed in small communities rather than in the resource provider that supports it. If I thought like the world, our ten-story building downtown and its many hundred square feet of appendages along more than a city block would be the best representation of the kingdom. But it's not. The kingdom is more real in my living room than in my office.

That's one of the great mysteries of the kingdom.

Today the world is seeing the power of religious zealots in small groups living for a mission. Their mission has been disruption and destruction, and their actions have reordered the world and how we relate to one another, to storekeepers, to airline security, and to people who show up at the front door unannounced. For those in such movements, their twisted religion is their life. For too many Christians, though, their faith is little more than a hobby.

What if, instead, Christians lived like Jesus taught—committed to and passionate about the in-breaking kingdom of God. What if they were working in small groups, perhaps organized by their church or informally connected at their workplace, asking the question, "How can we do kingdom work right here, right now?"

When you are on a kingdom mission, you are in some ways establishing an embassy of sorts, to use a diplomatic term. You are involved in making the invisible kingdom of God break through to become visible through the work of the kingdom in that time and that place. You are representing God in an alien land. So . . .

From now on, then, we do not know anyone in a purely human way. Even if we have known Christ in a purely human way, yet now we no longer know Him like that. Therefore, if anyone is in Christ, he is a new creation; old things have passed away, and look, new things have come.

Everything is from God, who reconciled us to Himself through Christ and gave us the ministry of reconciliation: That is, in Christ, God was reconciling the world to Himself, not counting their trespasses against them, and He has committed the message of reconciliation to us.

Therefore, we are ambassadors for Christ; certain that God is appealing through us. We plead on Christ's behalf, "Be reconciled to God." He made the One who did not know sin to be sin for us, so that we might become the righteousness of God in Him. (2 Cor. 5:16–21)

We represent a sovereign King from another kingdom, propagating his good news in the kingdom of this world. We don't belong here, but we do have work to do here. And the most significant percentage of it will not be in huge, stadium-filled ways but in small, primarily unnoticed ways. Very simple. Very sincere. Very understated. Very subversive.

4. We show and share the love of Christ. We've talked often about the proclamation and demonstration of the gospel. *Both matter.* But sometimes we say that sharing Christ and serving the community in the name of Christ are two sides of the same coin. This is a bad metaphor, though, because it implies that those two sides have to be flipped one to the other. God's mission is not two things; it is one thing—it is joining Jesus on mission as his ambassador. Some parts of those functions are given to the church gathered and some to the church scattered. But God's people are called to live for Jesus' kingdom mission. The church is called to "make disciples" while also "teaching them to observe everything" Jesus commanded us (Matt. 28:19–20), leading all believers to lead kingdom-shaped lives.

5. *We live our lives in a manner directed by (and empowered by) our King.* Jesus calls us to live our personal lives, as well our lives with other believers, by following a different code of ethics than the world and its ungodly kingdom principles. We are meant to be noticeable not just because of the way we talk or things we oppose but rather by the high standards with which we operate.

We will seem odd when we do this sometimes, but don't all residents from other countries seem different at first? Yes, they live here and put down roots here, but they still represent and bear certain loyalties to another place. And so do we. Our lives are radically different because we refuse to adopt and embrace the values of a world in rebellion to our God and King.

Yet we do not accomplish this daily endeavor in our own strength. Jesus not only gives us his teaching but also his Spirit to work in us and draw people's attention toward the Son. The end result is subversive, countercultural living. It shows other people what a difference his kingdom makes.

6. We wait for this lost, broken world to be completely fixed and reconciled to God. Yes, the kingdom is "already," but it is still "not yet." Complete victory is inaugurated but it is not yet consummated. And even though Christ's conquest is ultimately assured, right now the battle rages back and forth, delaying the end until the time set by God himself.

And I'll just say it. I'm about ready for this to end.

Not long ago my father e-mailed me about my sister, who died from a rare form of cancer while she was in college. His message arrived during the week of her birthday, when she would have been forty-five years old.

He said, "I miss her."

I e-mailed back, "I miss her too, Dad."

We are waiting for a day when these things do not happen anymore.

Some time ago I tweeted about the tragic suicide of a member of my extended family, ending my post with the word, "Come quickly, Lord Jesus." Someone asked me, "Why did you say that? How are those things connected?" They're connected because our citizenship is in heaven. We wait in hope for the return of our Savior. Right now our broken world rebels against its rightful king. People get sick. People are hurt. People hurt each other. People die.

Yes, the kingdom of God has come near, and our families and churches are outposts for the kingdom of God. We experience the kingdom's power, and we work to subvert the world's system and see the advance of God's glorious kingdom, where people are transformed, marriages are restored, and relationships are reconciled. We will never, however, take over the world and fix all its problems. So we look to Jesus, and we wait in hope.

The writer of the letter to the Hebrews said, "Since we are receiving a kingdom that cannot be shaken, let us hold on to grace" (12:28). As we are receiving this kingdom, it is an action in process, not completed. The word *shaken* in this verse comes from a word meaning unmoved, firm, and stable. It also is used in Acts 27:41, where it refers to a ship run aground with "the bow jammed fast . . . unmovable."

Often it seems circumstances in our world are always changing—most often for the worse. What God is doing in his kingdom, however, is creating a place of stability and firmness for a people who currently yet temporarily live in the midst of chaos. He calls us to join him in destroying the devil's works and establishing more and more outposts of his righteous kingdom. And as our Lord delivers this kingdom to us, our lives fairly shout our testimony to the reality of the unmovable, unshakable God.

"Fear not, little flock; for it is your Father's good pleasure to give you the kingdom" (Luke 12:32 KJV). He has. He will. And its subversive nature changes you, those around you, and ultimately the world.

The kingdom of God is among you.

Stay subversive.

Notes

Chapter 1

1. Richard Lovelace, *Renewal as a Way of Life* (Eugene, OR: Wipt & Stock Publishers, 2002), 47.

Chapter 2

1. C. S. Lewis, *The Weight of Glory* (New York, NY: HarperCollins, 2001).

Chapter 3

1. Philip Yancey, *The Jesus I Never Knew* (Grand Rapids, MI: Zondervan, 2002), 275.

2. Tullian Tchividjian, *Unfashionable* (Colorado Springs, CO: Multnomah, 2009), 53.

3. Gary Haugen, *Good News about Injustice* (Downers Grove, IL: Intervarsity Press, 1999), 48.

Chapter 4

1. See http://www.poets.org/viewmedia.php/prmMID/ 21414, accessed August 8, 2011.

2. James Davidson Hunter, *To Change the World: The Irony, Tragedy, and Possibility of Christianity in the Late Modern World* (New York, NY: Oxford, 2010).

Chapter 6

1. See http://www.compassion.com/default.htm. My family and I "adopted" a child, Blanca, in a village in Honduras to provide support not just for her but for sustainable development in her community. I want my children to learn and care about the poor so we pray, write letters, and give. We're teaching them kingdom values.

2. From Kiva's "About" page at http://www.kiva.org: "We are a nonprofit organization with a mission to connect people through lending to alleviate poverty. Leveraging the Internet and a worldwide network of microfinance institutions, Kiva lets individuals lend as little as $25 to help create opportunity around the world. Learn more about how it works."

Right now, I am an "investor" in businesses in Kyrgyzstan, Mongolia, Benin, the Philippines, and Rwanda. I believe such ventures lift people from poverty, not just provide them a temporary escape. I like to think of myself as a global business mogul helping to alleviate global poverty. By the way, you don't have to take back the funds when they are repaid—we just reinvest in another poor community.

3. Denominations are one of the best ways to give; they

already have people on the ground and in the field, often with local believers in partnership.

Chapter 7

1. Wayne Cordeiro, *The Irresistible Church: 12 Traits of a Church Heaven Applauds* (Minneapolis, MN: Bethany House Publishers, 2011), 100.

2. Tertullian, *On Adultery* (Whitefish, MO: Kessinger Publishing, 2004), 3.

3. Taken from the author's notes of Tim Keller's address at the 2009 Gospel Coalition.

4. Reggie McNeal, *Missional Renaissance: Changing the Scorecard for the Church* (San Francisco, CA: Jossey-Bass, 2009), 45.

5. See http://religion.blogs.cnn.com/2010/12/23/my-take-why-my-church-rebelled-against-the-american-dream, accessed September 14, 2011.

6. See http://www.summitrdu.com/index.cfm/PageID /1654/index.html, accessed September 14, 2011.

7. See http://www.samaritanspurse.org/index.php/articles/ small_church_big_heart, accessed September 14, 2011.

8. Trevin Wax, *Holy Subversion: Allegiance to Christ in an Age of Rivals* (Wheaton, IL: Crossway, 2010), 149.

Chapter 8

1. Lesslie Newbigin, *The Open Secret: An Introduction to the Theology of Mission* (Grand Rapids, MI: Eerdmans, 1978), 6–7.

2. See http://www.interpretermagazine.org/interior. asp?ptid=43&mid=13721, accessed October 10, 2011.

3. David Wells, *God in the Wasteland: The Reality of Truth in a World of Fading Dreams* (Grand Rapids, MI: Eerdmans, 1994), 114.

4. Ibid., 115.

Chapter 9

1. Wolfgang Simson, *Houses That Change the World* (Waynesboro, GA: Authentic Media, 2003), xxvi–xxviii.

Chapter 10

1. See http://missionvancouver.com/missionvancouver. html, accessed October 14, 2011.

ON MISSION. WITH GOD.
WHEREVER YOU ARE.

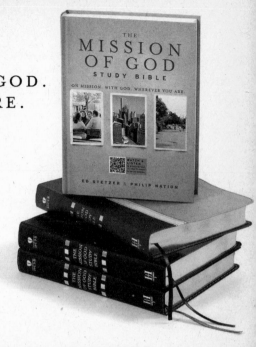

**WATCH &
LISTEN**
to presentations
on what it means
to be on mission.

DISCOVER CONTRIBUTIONS FROM

MATT CHANDLER, BILLY GRAHAM, JACK HAYFORD, ERWIN LUTZER, R.C. SPROUL, AND MORE.

The Mission of God Study Bible is designed to encourage followers of Jesus Christ to see their everyday life from God's perspective and have His heart for people. It's a reminder that we live around people in desperate need of redemption and reconciliation with God, which can only be found in Jesus.

Readers will hear from many of today's top thinkers, theologians, and leading voices in the church about what it means to live in the mission of God. Essay contributors include Matt Chandler, Tullian Tchividjian, Ed Stetzer, Linda Bergquist, Dave Ferguson, Christopher J.H. Wright, Matthew Barnett and many others.

Readers will also discover "Letters to the Church" from elder statesmen that will speak to the grand narrative of God's mission in Scripture. Letters from Billy Graham, Jack Hayford, Erwin Lutzer, Calvin Miller and R.C. Sproul will inspire you to live God's mission daily. Gaining God's Perspective and Heart for People. Wherever You Are.

MissionOfGodStudyBible.com

HCSB

HOLMAN
BIBLE PUBLISHERS